HISTORY OF SCOTLAND

A Journey Through Scottish History, the Battles, Clans, Highlanders, Myths, and Legends, Including Robert Bruce; William Wallace; Mary, Queen of Scots & Many More

HISTORY BROUGHT ALIVE

HISTORY OF SCOTLAND

FREE BONUS FROM HBA: EBOOK BUNDLE

Greetings!

First of all, thank you for reading our books. As fellow passionate readers of History and Mythology, we aim to create the very best books for our readers.

Now, we invite you to join our VIP list. As a welcome gift, we offer the History & Mythology Ebook Bundle below for free. Plus you can be the first to receive new books and exclusives! Remember it's 100% free to join.

Simply scan the QR code to join.

<u>**Keep up to date with us on:**</u>

YouTube: History Brought Alive

Facebook: History Brought Alive

www.historybroughtalive.com

CONTENTS

INTRODUCTION

The history of Scotland is nuanced. There are more complexities to this nation's past than many are first led to believe. The Scottish people are sometimes shown to be rough or unsophisticated, and there are stereotypes about their culture. To break away from these fixed ideas, a deeper understanding of who they are as a people is required. Delving into their background is the best way to gain a solid foundation about their national identity.

Looking at the past of this nation makes many historians present their history with a nationalistic twist. In other words, they tend to make the Scots seem like downtrodden examples of virtue. Others might make them seem like a bullied people who have had to deal with a constant threat to their sovereignty on their southern border. While there may be truth to some of this, it's more helpful to gain an objective perspective upon which to base further understanding. Productive dialogue will be the result.

With objectivity in mind, this book presents the history of the Scottish people in a neutral fashion. Where events in other countries are provided, it's to place local Scottish developments into better perspective. The mention of independence of the country at multiple points of the book should be interpreted as providing information as to the country's level of autonomy, not to advocate for or against higher levels of self-rule. The priority of the book will be to provide an overview of the adventures, battles, people, and periods that came to define the Scots.

With the aim of proper understanding in mind, this book is broken into five chapters that each cover a different era. The first covers prehistory, the Roman conquests, and the kingdoms of the Britons, Picts, and Scotti tribes. Information that's devoid of myth as much as possible to debunk misconceptions is provided. The purpose of this is to give an accurate prehistorical picture. This is followed by the era of the Scottish kingdom in the second chapter.

The unification of the Scotti, Picts, and Britons into the kingdom of Alba is examined in depth. This kingdom was the predecessor of the kingdom of Scotland and as such is a necessity for historical education. The progression of the kingdom of Scotland's rulers along with the events that provide context to their rule is then examined in the third chapter. The Renaissance and Scottish Reformation are two such events. The final chapters of the book will give you an overview of the unification of the crowns and parliaments of England and Scotland, followed by the developments of a modernizing Scotland from the start of the Industrial Revolution to present.

Books published by History Brought Alive are well written and thoroughly researched. The resources used are reliable and will provide you with accurate information. We have a large catalogue of books that are loved and read by many. This book is no different. You will be provided with information that is interesting, detailed, and well-rounded about the periods of this nation's history. This includes prehistory, ancient history, the Medieval periods, and the modern era. Don't waste your time and energy on confusing and ineffective books. You have the answers you need right here.

CHAPTER 1
THE EARLY HISTORY OF SCOTLAND

The history of Scotland stretches back before written records. There are archeological records stretching back thousands of years. In this chapter, we're going to explore Scotland from its earliest prehistory right up to the birth of the kingdoms of the Picts and Britons at the start of the Early Middle Ages.

PREHISTORIC SCOTLAND

It's assumed that people crossed the English Channel during the Paleolithic period (between 12,000 and 10,800 B.C.E.). The channel wasn't filled with water because the Ice Age had stored enough of the water in ice sheets for the sea level to drop. The crossings were believed to have been made from France. No structures from this period are available to study, likely due to the inhabitants having been hunter-gatherers who only settled temporarily in different locations.

With the ending of the Ice Age around 10,000–9,500 B.C.E., Scotland was heavily wooded, making it ideal for hunting small animals and foraging. Flints have been found by rivers, along the coast, and in caves, indicative of their hunting practices.

The Mesolithic period, or Middle Stone Age, ranged from around 10,800 to 4,100 B.C.E. in Scotland. Therefore, there was a slight overlap between the Mesolithic and the later Paleolithic periods. The Middle Stone Age is distinguished by stone tools that were slightly less crude and the use of microliths (small flints used to make arrowheads, spearheads, and tool attachments). The tools used also expanded to other substances, such as antlers, bone, and wood. Structures of the time were typically made with a wooden frame and weren't very large.

People's diets included a variety of foods, ranging from fish and animals to berries and nuts. The people of the Mesolithic period also started farming on a very small scale by making small clearings in the trees. Fishing became more common with the introduction of hooks. This combined with their predominantly hunter-gatherer lifestyle to make a more well-rounded diet, as evidenced by archeological finds of camp waste. The waste includes charred hazelnut shells, fish bones, and burnt wood. These waste dump sites are called middens and contain a wealth of information about the prehistoric peoples' way of life, even if the organic material present in the middens has long since deteriorated.

The earliest settlement in Scotland that we know about was at Cramond. The site is dated back to around 8,500 B.C.E. and can be found outside the village of Echline. The firepit in the middle runs 23 ft long and 1.6 ft deep. It's surrounded by hearths on which inhabitants could relax to absorb the warmth of the flames at night or during cold days.

Holes in the earth around the location indicate that upright posts were present to make walls. The walls were likely covered with animal skins and the roof made from turf. The community was hunted for at least some of its food sources, as shown by flint arrowheads that were found by archeologists.

The Neolithic people (people of the New Stone Age) brought the development of farming with them. This period stretched from around 4,100 to 2,500 B.C.E. in Scotland. One of the most distinctive characteristics of this period is that permanent structures and settlements were much more common than before. Instituting farming was likely the cause because individuals could rely on the same pieces of land for their food sources over periods lasting years. Large forest areas were cleared around 3,000 B.C.E. to make space for the farmland of locals following this new way of life.

Some believe that the farming was developed by people locally, but a large number of historians state that the farmers traveled from Europe to settle among the people already present from the earlier Stone Ages. The immigration combined with better food security resulted in a population increase. Hoe blades and other agricultural tools made farming more effective, resulting in even higher levels of food security.

There were multiple villages in Scotland that were established during this period. Skara Brae in Orkney is one such settlement. Another one that's perhaps better known is Calanais on the Isle of Lewis. Maeshowe is a third. These sites teach us a lot about the lives of those who lived thousands of years before us.

Further sites of interest are the permanent stone structures that the Neolithic people of Scotland made. This includes stone circles, tombs and cairns, megaliths, henges, and rock art panels. Archeological finds from this period show that stone was used for a large variety of purposes in addition to making structures. Things like axe heads, attachments to weapons, and carved stone balls have all been found. The purpose of these balls is not yet known; thus, we assume they were used for decorative purposes. They are unique to the British Isles, and a number of them were found in Scotland.

The next period in prehistoric development was the Bronze Age, which lasted from around 2,500 to 800 B.C.E. in Scotland. Metalworking arrived from the European mainland, altering multiple facets of life. Copper, bronze (combination of tin and copper), and gold were some of the first metals used. This is not to say that nonmetal substances weren't used for a variety of purposes. It's just that the introduction of metalwork was a game-changer that was widely incorporated.

Other materials used were amber, bone, wood, stone, antlers, clay, and a range of other natural substances. Metal, however, was used for a variety of functions in short order, as evidenced by hoards that have been found in Scotland. Hoards included jewelry, weapons, and tools.

Another characteristic of the Bronze Age was the change to the method of handling the dead. Both cremation and burial were used. However, burials took place both in groups and individually (often with personal trinkets), and the structures used for burials seemed to become simpler (such as the use of cists).

Other stone structures were also simplified and made more practical. This included hillforts and brochs (circular stone towers). Brochs are widespread in Scotland, with around 500 still remaining, even if just as foundations.

Although brochs are sometimes called Pictish towers, the era of the Picts only comes much later in prehistory.

The Bronze Age also showed an increase in warfare. This was possibly because of the ease and speed with which weapons could be produced. There may be other reasons that will never be known.

The Iron Age followed the Bronze Age, from around 800 B.C.E. to 400. During this age, weapons and tools became more effective due to iron being stronger than copper (and stronger than bronze when alloyed with other metals). The methods of processing iron would also have a large effect on the material's strength, with these methodologies being perfected as time progressed. In Scotland, the Iron Age also saw the arrival of the Celts and their way of life.

The Celts were a people who had spread all over Europe and in some of the Middle East. They were a collection of many tribes with individual identities. That said, even though each tribe was distinctive, there were similarities between them all. These included their pagan belief systems, their agricultural lifestyle, and often a hierarchical social structure. There seems to have been less of a hierarchical society in the early Celtic tribes of Scotland, as evidenced by communities with similar household styles and lack of a high degree of ornamentation. Some of the structures that abounded from the Celtic period of the Scottish Iron Age included wheelhouses, souterrains (underground storage chambers), forts, and ordinary stone houses.

The Romans arrived in the middle of this Celtic period—around 43. They were a warring empire set on conquering as much land and as many people as they could.

The tribes of Scotland and those from lower in Britain who had fled to Scotland put up too much of a challenge for the Romans. While the Romans did manage to conquer large parts of northern Britain, they weren't able to subdue the tribes for long periods of time.

To make matters simpler, Hadrian's Wall and the Antonine wall were built across the Central Belt. These kept the tribes that were too much trouble to conquer on the one side and the "civilized" conquered peoples on the other. The Central Belt had long been a point of transition between different Celtic peoples. Thus, the walls were erected along a convenient neck of the island that would solidify these location divides.

The Romans brought many things with them. Things such as board games, wine, glass vessels, and coins were all incorporated into the societies they had conquered. Through trade and other relations, the hardy tribes of Scotland gradually incorporated some of these Roman articles into their living, including the strong tribes of the Picts, Scotti, and Britons that gradually thrived to the north. That said, perhaps the biggest impact the Romans had on these tribes was the introduction of Christianity and Latin, both of which would increase in prominence after the end of the Iron Age.

The next section will take a deeper look at the Celts of the early and middle periods of the Iron Age.

THE ARRIVAL OF THE CELTS IN SCOTLAND

The Celts were a grouping of multiple peoples of the prehistoric world. They stretched across much of Europe, including the British Isles. The people were united by the similarity of their languages and their tribal nature, use of an economy that was based mainly on agriculture (or sometimes mining and artisanry alongside farming), and social hierarchies.

The society of the Celts in Scotland during the Iron Age was arranged as farmsteads, villages, or hamlets with multiple family households. The society seemed to be more flat than that in other Celtic regions, that is, their hierarchy was less prominent. This is due to multiple homesteads of a similar nature often being built close to one another, as assumed by historians. The society would likely have been competitive, and there was little to no need for an overarching governmental or ruler class from around the sixth to first centuries B.C.E.

The amount of farming during the last few centuries B.C.E. was higher than before. Financial wealth was an effect of this, resulting in families forming powerful dynasties. An artifact—silver chains weighing multiple pounds—was indicative of this dynastic power. Other signs of an increase in wealth were that jewelry had become highly ornamental and seemed to be accessible to a large percentage of the population. The assumption is thus that there was a period of general affluence at the time.

During the conquest by the Roman Empire during the first century, the writer Ptolemy noted there were nine tribes who occupied the region. The following section expounds on them.

CALEDONES

This tribe consisted of people who were described as being red-haired and having large limbs. They were described as being fast and fierce, which resulted in the Romans never fully conquering them. The name of the tribe translates to "possessing hard feet," which could have alluded to their endurance or to the rocky land they lived on. The tribe was located in the tract of land that stretched from modern-day Fort William to Inverness.

A warlike people, the Caledones built hillforts and farmsteads fortified with earthworks. Their economy was largely made up by farming, and the settlements they lived in were scattered.

Smaller tribes that were included in the Caledones were the Carnonacae, Creones, and Smertae. The Smertae were believed to smear themselves with blood, either from sacrifices or from their enemies. Whether these tribes were all separate peoples who came together when mutual defense was needed or whether they shared a mutual leader is unknown. That said, they were a strong opponent for the invading Romans, and they even overcame part of Hadrian's Wall during the 180s. A peace treaty was signed with them, but they didn't keep to it, attacking Roman soldiers on multiple occasions.

Emperor Septimius Severus tried to gain dominance over them around 209, which turned out to be a success for him. After being defeated, the Caledones gave up part of their land to the Romans, which was then razed and made unusable. Even after defeat, the Caledones continued fighting, gradually eroding Roman troops with surprise attacks and help from other tribes. When Septimius Severus's son was sent to destroy them once and for all in 211, his own troops refused as they refused to acknowledge him as their emperor. The outcome of the intended destruction thus turned around, resulting in a peace treaty in which the Caledones gained back their lands. A century later, the Romans again campaigned into the north.

The Caledones were described as having red hair, just like the Picts. This has led some to believe that the Picts were a tribe that developed from the earlier Caledones.

DAMNONII

Damnonii translates to "the masters." Very little is known about this tribe other than their location. They were said to occupy parts of south-central Scotland and sections of the west coast. The Romans claimed to have conquered them and occupied their land during the invasions.

EPIDII

The region occupied by the Epidii was rocky and mountainous. Their name originates from a word for "horse," which links up with the presence of ponies and horses in the Highlands that are suited to rocky terrain. They were thought to have originated on the Islay and then to spread into northwest Scotland. A low population was a natural result of tough lands and living conditions, with the tribe being described as not having large numbers. The combination of the low population and irregular landscape meant that it wasn't worth it for the Romans to try to send troops to overcome, control, and tax the people of this tribe—there wouldn't have been a good return on investment.

NOVANTAE

The Novantae lived in what is today Dumfries and Galloway when the Romans first invaded. The lack of archeological finds of Roman military installations in the area denotes that there was likely a peaceable relationship between the tribe and the empire. Further marks of a peaceful relationship are the lack of tribal defense structures, despite two centuries of Roman occupation. The people of the Novantae were mainly herders and farmers.

SELGOVAE

This tribe occupied the south-central Highlands. Their name means "the hunters," and they were thought to be part of the Brythonic class of Celts. Their settlements were commonly made up of small forts with stone or wooden walls. The capital was a fortified hill town, but it was abandoned in 79 due to the presence of a Roman installation nearby. Several other towns and settlements were abandoned at the time, likely due to the intense combat that took place because of Roman troops being stationed throughout their lands. Despite the ever-present threat, the tribe grew in strength, reaching its height in the second century.

TAEXALI

The east of Scotland was occupied by this tribe. They lived on farms and hamlets that had few defenses. The way of life of the Taexali was peaceful and consisted of farming their fertile lands. The lack of defense made them a soft target, resulting in Roman conquest in 84. When the Roman forces retreated to the south of the Antonine Wall, the Taexali were once again able to take control of their lands to continue their pastoral way of life.

VACOMAGI

The Vacomagi tribe was located in what is today Moray, which is a mountainous area. Their name translates to "inhabitants of the curved fields," which shows that they were an agricultural tribe—much like their southerly neighbors, the Taexali. Very little is known about them.

VENICONES

This tribe was located in and around Fife, just south of the Taexali. This region was the best location from which the Romans could quell the attacks of other tribes, which meant the Venicones were soon dislocated so their land could be occupied more permanently by the Romans. The Venicones were perhaps a tribe who had fled north during the conquests of the regions that now make up England. Unique practices of the tribe were the use of bronze armlets that could weigh up to 3 lbs and burial in stone graves.

VOTADINI (ALSO OTADINI)

Archeological evidence at the Traprain Law hillfort establishes them as extant from at least the eighth century B.C.E., and the Traprain Treasures are attributed to the tribe. They occupied southeast Scotland and northeast England, living in hillforts and villages. Hadrian's Wall was built across the southernmost parts of their lands, while the Antonine Wall was erected across their northernmost territories. Some of the Votadini settlements and forts were incorporated as a support structure for the troops that manned the walls. It seems that the relationship between the tribe and the Romans was mainly peaceful, with the tribe continuing to occupy their own lands.

They became a powerful people, with one of their fifth-century kings (Cunedda) having aided the people of Wales in warfare. They also occupied the kingdom of Lothian from the third to seventh centuries, keeping their power strong until invasions by the Angles wore them down. The Angles overtook the lands of Lothian until Kenneth I MacAlpin regained the territory in the tenth century. The Gododdin were said to be the descendants of the Votadini.

Now that we've examined the nine tribes, we're going to look at the actions of the Romans. The next section dives into the invasion that took place and any effects it had on the people of the tribes over the long term.

THE ROMAN INVASION AND ITS IMPACT ON SCOTLAND

The Romans invaded and successfully conquered the peoples of England between the first century B.C.E. and the second century. They permanently left their mark on the people, including cultural, architectural, artistic, and commercial aspects. Commercial aspects included a continent-wide trade route that brought both goods and people from other parts of the empire. This allowed those living in the southern parts of Britain to build wealth and to take on a Romanized way of life. The same cannot be said about the tribes occupying what is now Scotland.

Many of the tribes of northern Britain made good soldiers. They were hardy people who knew the land they lived on and were willing to put up protracted opposition. The Romans saw them as uncivilized, and they saw the Romans as unnecessarily violent. During the first century, attempts were made to conquer the northern tribes. The Battle of Mons Graupius of 83 or 84 was the breakthrough the Romans were looking for.

Julius Agricola was a general at the time who personally participated in the attacks. He sent a fleet of ships as well as infantry to attack the opposition. The tribal forces who had previously always fled when conflict arose were now forced into a position where they had to attack or submit—they couldn't run away. This was because the Romans threatened the main food stocks of the Caledonian tribe, which could have left its people starving if left undefended. The forces faced the Romans, who closed in on them and forced them to flee to the trees.

The forces of the Romans followed them into the trees, and the result was the death of a third of the tribal forces— 10,000 people. The remaining 20,000 people couldn't be found the following day, and the general was lauded for having subdued the whole isle of Britain. That said, further campaigns were held into Scotland. The area was far removed from the heart of the Roman Empire.

The tribes renewed their vigor after the Battle of Mons Graupius, standing their own against the Romans. The Romans managed to gain control of many regions of the area, including islands off the coast of the Scottish mainland and parts of the Highlands. The cost of sustaining power over the region, however, was too high.

It was more economical to separate the savage northerly tribes from the subdued ones. A major contribution to this was likely the nonhierarchical structure of the tribes of the region. They could elect replacements for dead chiefs quickly, which meant that power vacuums didn't destabilize the tribes. The new chief would rekindle his forces, and the Romans had to continue providing manpower to sustain victories over the area. It was just too costly in relation to the benefits reaped.

The solutions were Hadrian's Wall (built in 122) and the Antonine Wall (built around 142). The walls were manned, and fortifications were put up along them. There were very few attempts at conflict other than some clashes along the border regions of the empire and tribal lands.

The tribes to the north unified to form a nation called the Picts, meaning "painted people" (due to the blue tattoos and paint they put on themselves). In 306, a campaign was held to strengthen protection against the tribes who were coming down to attack the wall. The campaign was led by the emperor Constantius Chlorus. Once the border was reaffirmed along Hadrian's Wall, the troops needed to return to the heart of the empire to protect it from growing threats.

The continued troubles in the empire meant that a growing threat of the Picts couldn't be combatted properly. The Picts broke past Hadrian's Wall in around 360, and the troops who were sent by Emperor Julian couldn't quash them fully. The Picts increased their power and were capable of asserting themselves further into the Roman territories of England. Things were getting more heated close to home for the Roman Empire, resulting in withdrawal of its troops altogether around 411.

The tribes of Scotland maintained their own cultural beliefs and practices throughout the Roman occupancy. There might have been some trade and other forms of interaction besides warfare, but Roman culture only started being adopted by the people of Scotland once the Roman soldiers left. The main cultural aspect that had been maintained was Christianity, use of Latin (such as on stone carvings), and incorporation of a more hierarchical cultural structure than before. These Roman legacies were partly due to the invasions the tribes were now making south into Romanized areas of England.

To protect themselves from these invasions, the people who lived in the south of Britain hired the Angles to protect them. This backfired, with the Angles soon taking the opportunity to overcome the people they had been hired to protect. Further, they also invaded the areas of the Scottish tribes in an attempt to increase their power there. This was successful in some areas.

To understand the full context of what was happening at the time, it's necessary to look at parallel developments. The tribes of the Scotti, the Picts, and the Britons will be examined in the following sections. They formed before the arrival of the Angles and would go on to develop into the Scottish kingdom over the next half millennium.

THE SCOTTI AND DALRIADA

The Scotti were a Gaelic-speaking people. The term Scotti was used by the Romans to describe the people of Ireland, where the Scotti were believed to originate from. This is based on myth, however, and little evidence has been found to state that the Scotti weren't descended from people who had been living in Scotland before their time. There are some structures and objects that are similar on both islands from the time period (the early first millennium), but this could be due to trade, alliances, or marriage offerings.

The first records of the Scotti show that they emerged around the fourth century. They continued existing until the ninth century, after which they merged with the Picts and some of the Britons to form the kingdom of Alba. Alba later changed into the kingdom of Scotland. In the first century they were recorded, the Scotti seem to have established long-distance trade routes. They had goods from the Mediterranean and Gaul, among other areas. If the myth of the crossing of a whole people from Ireland is based on fact, then some of these trade routes would have been well-established.

This kingdom was called Dalriada. Eventually the Scottish regions of Dalriada gained power, while the Irish regions lost theirs. There would have been a ruling class that controlled what is now County Antrim and Northern Ireland, as well as the Inner Hebrides and Argyll. The main stronghold of this kingdom was said to have moved from Ireland to Scotland during this period. Dalriada flourished for centuries. St. Columba is described as having brought Christianity to the kingdom and granted King Aidan his right to rule during the sixth century.

During the later part of the sixth century and the early part of the seventh, battles between rivals for the Scotti throne caused turmoil in the kingdom. Other battling and warfare were also common at the time. The Picts often attacked the Scotti, especially when they were encroaching on their territory. The Angles also brought conflict with them. The Scotti remained strong throughout this, gradually expanding east, further into the territory of the Picts.

The power of the kingdom started faltering in the middle of the seventh century. To prevent it from becoming too weak, Oswy (an English king) consolidated Dalriada as a part of his kingdom. Part of his justification was the religious right to rule. The monastery of Iona, which was the most influential at the time, had led some to believe that previous kings of Dalriada had been placed on the throne as unnatural leaders. As a result, the ruling family's authority lost some of its status, allowing another family dynasty to take its place.

The new dynasty grew its power strategically. Marriage alliances with the Picts were one of the ways in which the power of the family was consolidated. Irish Dalriada was eventually wiped out, possibly by the Vikings during the next two centuries. This consolidated the power of the kingdom even more with the central family dynasty. There might have been a colony of some of the remaining Dalriada kingdom who established themselves in Pictland. Coupling this with the regime of intermarriage, the two kingdoms started influencing each other more and more.

The power consolidation and the allied position with the Picts (some of the time) meant that the Scotti were able to expand their zone of power. The Britons, Angles, Irish, and Vikings exerted pressure on the kingdom, but its heightened strength meant that it was able to stand firm. Eventually, the kingdoms of the Picts and the Scotti merged under Kenneth I MacAlpin during the ninth century. This was the birth of Alba. The next section will give a better understanding of the Picts as the second major ethnic group that formed the kingdom.

THE PICTS

The origin of the Picts is unsure, but it's likely that they were established during the Iron Age. There's a possibility that they were the aboriginal people of Scotland or that they formed from Celtic tribes in Scotland already or that they were a Celtic people who had sailed from Scythia beyond the Black Sea. If the latter is to be believed, they sailed to Ireland, where they were refused, resulting in them sailing across the Irish Sea and settling to the north of the Britons.

The Picts were a strong tribe, and they raided the Britons to their south. One of the kings of the Britons, Marius, beat them in battle. After the battle he allowed them to settle in the far northeast of the island, where Caithness is now located. They didn't have women with them, however, so an agreement was made with the Scotti to their west that they be given women to marry. The condition of this agreement was that succession disputes would be resolved by referring to the female line. While all this might or might not be myth, a fact is that the Picts did use the matrilineal line when resolving succession matters.

The tribe started flourishing in the fourth century, a period of success that would last for centuries. The kingdom of the Picts at the time was made up of multiple subkingdoms or tribes that were loosely linked together. The tribes were made up of family groups who lived close to one another. These family groups and tribes would unite to protect the loose federation from opposing peoples during times of unrest. Gradual consolidation took place over time, with two dominant kingdoms resulting—the Dicalydones and the Verturiones (another name for Fortriu).

The kingdom of Fortriu (under King Bridei) expanded its borders and started subjugating other Picts, until a united nation was formed. This nation came to be known as Pictland. During the same century, the Anglo-Saxons started throwing their weight around and establishing power throughout Britain. The kingdom of Northumbria was such an Anglo-Saxon region and became the dominant force of southern Scotland.

Northumbria was too powerful for the Picts to resist, resulting in it becoming a vassal kingdom during the seventh century. This wasn't a permanent state of affairs, with the success of the Picts at the Battle of Dun Nechtain in 685. The result of the battle included more independence from Northumbria for the Picts.

Over the next century, the Picts did a lot of battle with the Scotti to their west. This continued to the end of the eighth century, when a Pictish prince was put on the throne of Dalriada. They weren't yet fully united as a kingdom, but relations became better, allowing both kingdoms to positively interact with each other.

When Kenneth I MacAlpin eventually unified the kingdoms in the ninth century, the term Pict started fading from use. Some myths say he slaughtered all of the Picts, but a far more likely reason is that the Picts were assimilated into the Scotti. The nobles of both kingdoms used customs that were more uniformly Scotti in nature, and the use of the Pictish language reduced, particularly with the focus on using Scots and Gaelic dialects in churches.

THE BRITONS

The Britons were initially a Celtic grouping from the regions of prehistoric England. They lost much of their land during the invasions of the Romans. Some of them stayed behind and became Romanized, while others settled in different regions of the island. One of the regions they were displaced to was to the north in what is now Scotland. They established kingdoms and tribes there, some of which would become strong and others fail.

With the invasions of the Anglo-Saxons starting in the fifth century, more warfare and displacement took place. One of the more powerful Briton kingdoms that was established in the process of this relocation was Dumbarton, which originally meant "the fortress of the Britons." Dumbarton was a place that allowed the Briton culture to boom, with the creation of art such as poetry, tales, and ballads. Distinctive jewelry, pottery, and other artifacts were also created at the time.

The next three subsections will give an overview of three of the more powerful Brittonic kingdoms that existed on or within the borders of modern-day Scotland.

RHEGED

This kingdom originated before the arrival of the Romans. It occupied northeast England, bordering on the region that Hadrian's Wall would be built on later. It remained intact through the Roman occupation and was powerful when the Romans left. It finally fell after the Anglo-Saxon invasions, with the Viking conquests having erased what remnants might have remained.

The kingdom consisted of an alliance of multiple Celtic tribes called the Brigantes. The location that's today the city of Carlisle is possibly attributable to this kingdom during the Iron Age. That said, there were few heavily populated settlements in the kingdom. This was largely due to the poor quality of the soil combined with the rocky and moored regions within it.

During the period leading up to the Anglo-Saxon invasions, Rheged split up into two kingdoms, North and South Rheged. The northern kingdom was able to expand its borders, annexing territory in what is today Dumfries and Galloway. The kingdom remained strong and, with the cushion of the southern kingdom, managed to remain strong for a long period during the Anglo-Saxon invasions, only falling in the seventh century.

DUMBARTON

Dumbarton was the only Brittonic kingdom that didn't fall when the Anglo-Saxons invaded. The Anglo-Saxons were positioned to its south, while the Picts were to its north. The kingdom retained its independence despite these two rival peoples being right on its doorstep. It even managed to remain intact during the Viking invasions.

The Viking invasions started around 866. They were composed of forces from the king of Dublin, Olaf the White, and his wife, Aud, who was the ruler of the Hebrides. The stronghold of Dumbarton was sacked during this time, with riches and people being taken to be sold in Ireland. In spite of this and the death of their king at the hands of the Picts, the Britons of Dumbarton remained extant, eventually being absorbed into other kingdoms.

KINGDOM OF STRATHCLYDE

This kingdom was founded around 450 and took up parts of northern England and southern Scotland. Its original name was Ystrad Clud, which was used until it changed to Strathclyde in the ninth century. The Damnonii were the main early constituent tribe of this kingdom, and its earliest rulers (that we know of) were Tudwal and Rhydderch.

More is known about this kingdom than some others of the time. Famous artifacts from the kingdom include Dyrnwyn (a magical sword), the Govan Stones, and the Govan Sarcophagus. The religion of Strathclyde was Christianity, likely under the influence of the mother church in Iona. They followed the Leges inter Brettos et Scottos (the Laws of the Britons and Scots) and were the home to the majority of the Britons after the destruction of Dumbarton.

The kingdom of Northumbria posed continual problems to Strathclyde as it was the dominant kingdom in the region surrounding Strathclyde. It was not, however, the Northumbrians who brought down Strathclyde, but the Vikings, who destroyed its capital in 870. The remnants of the kingdom were absorbed into other Anglo-Saxon kingdoms in the tenth century and then leased to the Scots king Malcolm I in 945. When the Scots defeated the Anglo-Saxons at Carham during the eleventh century, the region was absorbed into the Scottish kingdom.

With a thorough foundation about the earliest periods of Scottish history, you are now ready to look into the developments of the Middle Ages. The next chapter will be dedicated to developments of the Medieval times, including the invasions of the Angles and Vikings and the rise of Alba and Scotland.

CHAPTER 2
THE MEDIEVAL PERIOD

The Middle Ages lasted from around 400 to 1500. This period is split into three main parts: the Early Medieval Period (around 400–1000), the High Medieval Period (1000–1300), and the Late Medieval Period (1300–1500). The Early Medieval Period is sometimes called the Dark Ages because of a lack of written sources that have lasted from that period, not because of a lack of development or a backward way of life. This means that we mainly use archaeological evidence or sources written during the later periods for information from this time.

The invasions of the Anglo-Saxons and the Vikings took place during the Early Medieval Period, while the Roman invasions withdrew from Britain. Many churches, hillforts, Pictish stones, and castles were erected during this era. Christianity gained prevalence, while paganism lost much of its presence. The kingdoms of the Scotti and Picts became more prominent, and they united during the latter part of this period.

The High Middle Ages were when the kingdom of Scotland went through much of its initial growth. It stopped being called Alba and formed a union of multiple cultures into one identity. The monarchy gained power, and the First War of Scottish Independence took place.

The Late Middle Ages were marked by an increase in the number of monasteries and cathedrals being built, as well as its first university. Central control of the government was firmly established, including tax and trade. Burghs were established and answerable to the monarchy. The end of the Late Middle Ages was when the Scottish Renaissance started to flourish.

THE ANGLO-SAXONS

When the Romans left Britain, it left the people to the south open to attacks and raids from the Picts, Scots, and other northern tribes. The Angles were asked to provide protection so that those in the south of Britain could retain the comfortable lifestyle they held when the Romans provided protection. The Angles were a Germanic people from the border region of modern Denmark and Germany. They had a militant nature and could be powerful foes. Thus, instead of providing protection to those in southern Britain, the Angles invaded to claim Britain for their own benefit.

They went ahead to conquer the southern regions (Roman Britannia) and then formulated seven kingdoms to their benefit. This arrangement was called the Heptarchy, that is, "rule of seven." These kingdoms were formed during the fifth century, and they remained extant until the invasions of the Vikings in the ninth century, when a majority of them were destroyed or rearranged.

Two of the northernmost kingdoms of the Heptarchy were Bernicia to the north of Hadrian's Wall and Deira directly to the south of Bernicia. The placement of Bernicia was right on the border of multiple tribes of Celtic origin, with contest over the territory during the sixth and seventh centuries. It managed to annex multiple areas from the Britons, including Dun Eideann. It also took possession of Deira along with parts of Mercia (located in the center of modern England) to form the kingdom of Northumbria. Northumbria became the preeminent kingdom of its area.

This power was finally checked with the invasion of the Vikings. They lost much of their influence, eventually being captured. During this time, Alba captured Dun Eideann. Eventually Alba took most of Northumberland in 1018 after conflict with the Vikings and the remaining Anglo-Saxons.

VIKING INVASIONS

The Vikings first raided the coast of Scotland around 793, including the raid of the monastery of Iona in 795. They established strongholds in the northwest regions of Scotland and on multiple islands surrounding Britain. They were a formidable sea people, and as such, they were able to take towns and land on the coast and claim said towns for themselves. Resources were taken from conquered lands or raided areas to be traded all over Europe. Vikings largely left their Northern European homes for reasons such as increased population and a lack of desired local resources.

Churches and castles were thus prime candidates for raids. Churches weren't always heavily protected, and they contained lots of valuable objects. Castles, while sometimes more difficult to access, contained many valuables and were a good source of animals and people to trade. Not all these raids were recorded, and archeological evidence isn't always easy to find as raids could sometimes be fast and often resulted in minimal destruction to fixed property. As the threat of the Vikings grew, people started preparing. They were willing to protect their assets, even if it came to violence or even if it meant that they would be placed in hidden hoards.

The British Isles were one of the nearer areas available for conquest and raiding to the Vikings. It was easily accessible by boat, and there was a wealth of natural and man-made resources available. The lands they took in northern Britain were mainly in the west, which left the Picts relatively undisturbed. Although they were both strong groups of people with military capacity, they were able to coexist to some extent.

THE RISE OF THE SCOTTISH KINGDOM

When the Scotti and Picts came together under the rule of Kenneth I MacAlpin in 843, the kingdom of Alba was born. At first it wasn't very large, occupying northeast Scotland. That said, the combination of the strengths of the Picts and the Scotti meant that not even the Vikings could subdue the newly unified kingdom. When the Vikings started withdrawing from the region, Alba expanded. Multiple surrounding territories were conquered in battles, such as during the Battle of Carham of 1018. King Malcolm II stopped English forces from the south and annexed the province of Lothian to the kingdom.

Malcolm II's successor was Duncan I, who took power in 1034. His reign resulted in massive expansions of the kingdom. Cumbria and Strathclyde were officially absorbed into Alba. After this unification, the name Scotland started being used more and more for the kingdom, while Alba was used less and less. Even though the term Alba was still sometimes used to describe Scotland, after the eleventh century, this name was used much less.

When William the Conqueror took England, this posed a threat to Alba. The new English kingdom had robust military capacity and a lot of wealth. However, this danger was largely reduced after signing the Treaty of Falaise, which was ratified in 1175. The treaty stated that the English king would be seen as the overlord of Scotland. This meant that Scotland would have to pay him certain amounts for the use of the land it was on in line with the feudal system.

The feudal system consisted of a king or overlord granting management of land to nobles in return for their allegiance, and the nobles would in turn grant use of that land and protection to tenants. In return for this use, the tenants would provide rent, labor, and farmed goods, among other things, to the noble. With the ratification of this treaty, the king of England was the feudal overlord, and the king of Scotland was one of the subjects to whom he granted management of land.

One of the implications of this treaty was that Scotland was no longer preoccupied with protecting itself from England. It could focus on agriculture, commerce, and its own affairs—so long as it provided military support and other defined benefits to England. As such, the economy of Scotland grew, which in turn increased the power of the church. The church was directly involved in the lives of its members, providing both a commercial and social center, along with religious guidance. People donated to the church and paid tithes, which was one of the reasons it became so important as an institution in later times. It worked hand in hand with the government (i.e., the monarchy) to manage Scottish society.

The next section will give summaries of the lives and impacts of the first kings of Alba up to the start of the tenth century. This will provide a better context of the lives of the Scottish people and the events they were confronted with during the last parts of the Early Middle Ages.

KINGS OF ALBA

Kenneth I MacAlpin

The king to unify a nation, Kenneth I MacAlpin was the son of a king of the Scots clans of the Gaels. His father had military success against the Picts. Kenneth took on the position of ruler of the Picts, establishing himself firmly as their leader over a period of more than 15 years. He expanded his Pictish territory through conquest and possibly with marriage.

The unification of the Pictish and Scotti territories over a protracted period gradually formed the beginning of a joint identity. Both the Picti and the Scotti were tribes that were descended from the Celts. Kenneth died around 850, leaving his brother to take over his position to consolidate the regions Kenneth had conquered.

Donald I

Following the founder of a kingdom is never easy. Donald I was in the tough position of succeeding his brother, who had founded Alba and fought to establish its power. He wasn't as popular as his brother because he had a slightly blithe personality and his mother was foreign. That said, he consolidated the power of the kingdom and prevented it from splitting into parts (as many kingdoms did soon after being founded).

He established the use of tanistry (election of a king or chief by their extended eligible family) to ensure certainty about the process for appointing new successors. This would mean not only that the best of the possible candidates was chosen (i.e., the most persuasive and powerful) but also that there wouldn't be a shortage of replacements when a king died. A monarch didn't need to have children to ensure a successor was in place, and the crown wouldn't be given to someone too feeble to protect the nation.

Constantine I

Not much of Constantine's period as king of the Picts and Scots (from 863 to 877) was recorded in writing. The majority of what we know consists of legend. The period was a turbulent one, with the Dublin-based Danish king instigating raids into Pictland and the land of the Scots each year. The southern areas of Northumberland and Galloway were also under constant attack, with the commander of the Great Heathen Army (Halfdan Ragnarsson) perpetrating the attacks. The king was constantly on the lines of battle, eventually dying while combating raiders to the north.

Aed

Aed, who was one of the sons of Kenneth I McAlpin, became the king of Picts. He assumed the throne in 877 and was killed in 878. He was a feeble king who had failed to protect Pictland from the Viking invasions, resulting in widespread loss of wealth and anarchy. The commoner, Giric, was a refugee of the Viking invasions and managed to gain favor with Aed. With Eochaid as his accomplice, Giric got rid of Aed, and they took on the throne of Pictland together.

Eochaid and Giric

These joint monarchs ruled from 878 to 889. The relationship between the two is unclear, but it is clear that Giric played an integral part in making it possible for Eochaid to take the throne and that the period of their rule wasn't the most peaceable of times. Eochaid was the son of the king of Strathclyde and the nephew of King Aed. They managed to get rid of Aed and took the crown for themselves.

During the early part of their reign, Giric got rid of any Picts in the court who could pose a threat to their rule. In their stead, Giric installed loyal Scotti in the court. He could not, however, dispatch the two biggest threats to the throne—the two Pictish sons of Aed. They were safely in exile under the protection of their aunt, who had married an Irish king. The sons were Donald and Constantine, who both would go on to rule the nation after Giric and Eochaid.

At that point in time, there was still a clear delineation between the Scots and the Picts, with the crown serving as joint rule over both Celtic groups. Their reign came to an end when Eochaid enlisted the help of his nephew Donald to dispose of Giric. After disposing of him, Donald realized that he could seize the crown for himself, so he drove Eochaid out of the kingdom.

Donald II

Donald was the king of the Scots whose reign lasted from 889 to 900. He reigned during a turbulent period wherein the Danes and some tribes of the Highlands raided the kingdom. Not much is known about his death, but what is known is that his brother, Constantine II, was his successor. What makes his reign most notable, however, is that the Picts stopped being mentioned during this time. This was likely due to their assimilation into the national identity of the Scots, but history is unclear on this fact.

MONARCHS OF SCOTLAND UNTIL THE FIRST WAR OF SCOTTISH INDEPENDENCE

While Scotland was still sometimes called Alba, there was a gradual transition to the use of the word Scotland, or the kingdom of the Scots, starting around the end of Donald II's reign. This next section summarizes the lives of Scottish kings from this time to the end of the High Middle Ages.

Constantine II

The rule of Constantine II was the longest of any Scottish king during the tenth century. He reigned from 900 to 943 and retired to the position of monk until his death in

954. When he assumed the throne, the largest threat to the kingdom seemed to be the Norse, who had invaded and caused a lot of destruction throughout Alba during the first few years of his reign. He managed to drive them out during his fourth year as king. This drew the attention of the Danish king of Dublin (Rognvald), who laid waste to the town of Dunblane.

Constantine II was able to muster and strengthen his forces to face Rognvald and his allies, resulting in victory for the Scots at the River Tyne a few years later. After this the Norse were no longer a persistent threat to the kingdom, and he was able to focus his forces on the West Saxon kingdom in the south. To deal with the threat that was steadily encroaching on Scottish lands, he enlisted the help of other kingdoms in Britain. They were, however, solidly defeated by their powerful southern foe, with four of the kings dying, as well as one of Constantine II's sons.

When he returned to Scotland after the defeat, he abdicated, and the crown moved to Malcolm I. His reign included nonmilitary changes, the major one being the incorporation of the Church of Scotland, which had not been allowed to form by the earlier Pictish kings of Alba. Further, he managed to install his brother as the king of Strathclyde, thus resulting in a closer tie between the kingdoms, bringing the Britons of that kingdom closer to the kingdom of the Scots. As such, while his reign ended with a defeat from the West Saxons, he managed to secure his kingdom from Norse attacks, to gain allegiance with other kingdoms around the Scots, and to establish a national church.

Malcolm I

When Constantine II abdicated to become a monk in 943, Malcolm (who was his cousin) was elected to be king. His reign resulted in the expulsion of the Danes from York (which was under Scots authority at that point), obtaining Cumbria in the north. Northern parts of the kingdom were lost to the kingdom of West Saxony, which occupied parts of what is today England and the islands to the west of Britain. During the same year when Malcolm lost the northern territories of his kingdom (954), he was killed during a rebellion in Moray.

Indulf

His reign lasted for eight years from 954 to 962. He was the successor of Malcolm I and the son of Constantine II. He was a strong leader in warding off the Vikings, protecting his people from incursions both from the sea and over land. His military prowess led to the capture of Edinburgh and Lothian in what is now southern Scotland. He then went on to defeat the king of the Danes, Eric of the Bloody Axe, in battle. He intended to abdicate the throne and become a monk, but it's unsure whether this happened or whether he died before carrying out his intentions.

Dub

Dub was the son of Malcolm I and the successor of Indulf. He ruled from 962 to 967. His reign was during a time with very little record keeping and a lot of mythological twists to events; thus, not much can be said about him for certain. He was the brother of Kenneth II and the father of Kenneth III. During his reign there was some warfare, in which it is possible that he gained lands in central Scotland.

It's thought that he was killed on the orders of Culen, his successor.

Culen

Not a king to make any particularly lasting progress for the nation, Culen held the throne from 967 to 971. He was the son of Indulf, yet Dub was elected to the position of king instead of him. He contested this through conflict with Dub and the (assumed) orders to kill him. When he became king after Dub's death, he occupied himself with attempts to overcome the kingdom of Strathclyde for the purpose of subjugation. This was, however, unsuccessful. The king of Strathclyde (Riderch) went on to kill Culen in 971, likely as revenge for Culen killing Riderch's brother and raping his daughter.

Kenneth II

One of the longest periods of rule of the tenth century was that of Kenneth II. He reigned from 971 to his death in 995. The early part of his rule was characterized by a lot of warfare. Strathclyde and Northumbria were two of his main areas of conquest, with the aim being to obtain as much land as possible between the rivers Tweed and Forth for the Scots. He is believed to have acknowledged the English king Edgar as the Scottish overlord. In exchange, it is believed he received all the land between the two rivers—the land was called Lothian at the time.

He married an Irish princess with whom he had Malcolm II. His marital tie to Ireland served to strengthen his kingdom's position in Great Britain, which was composed of multiple kingdoms at the time. The later years of his rule were greatly concerned with expanding the kingdom northward, with attempts at obtaining lands in Orkney and Moray. These attempts were largely unsuccessful at the time of his murder, but the southern possessions of the kingdom were secure.

Constantine III

Constantine III had been elected to the throne when his predecessor had been killed in 995. His predecessor (Kenneth II) was his cousin. He reigned for two years, after which he, too, was killed.

Kenneth III

Kenneth held the throne for around eight years. He is thought to have obtained it by killing his predecessor. He was not entirely a usurper, being the son of Dub, who had been the king of Alba. His descendants were believed to include the mother of Macbeth. As he had done with his predecessor, his successor had him killed before taking the throne.

Malcolm II

Obtaining the throne by force in 1005, Malcolm II killed Kenneth III to take his place. He was a ruler who made use of military force, obtaining victory over Northumbria in 1016 to extend the domination of the Scottish kingdom. He also managed to gain control of Strathclyde, which he gave to his grandson (Duncan I) to rule. He tried to get around the succession process for his successor so that the throne would go to his grandson as well. He succeeded, but in doing so, it laid the groundwork for the violence that ensued with Macbeth and Duncan's son, Malcolm III Canmore. Other than the violence that would come, Malcolm II was known for his long reign (lasting until 1034) and for expanding the

Scottish borders to a size that almost corresponds with the Scotland of today.

Duncan I

Having a relatively short reign of only six years, Duncan had the favor of his grandfather (King Malcolm II). Strathclyde had been a region that had been outside the power of the Scottish kingdom before the reign of Malcolm II. Upon gaining power of the region, the king granted it to Duncan to rule, which was against the custom of the time.

Further, when Malcolm II died, he nominated Duncan as his heir, which further violated custom. The system in place at the time would have given the rule to someone in an alternate branch of the royal family, which is one of the reasons Macbeth rose up against Duncan within the first few years of his rule—Macbeth being from the other branch. To protect his power, Duncan went on the offensive and laid siege to Macbeth's lands. This didn't deter Macbeth, who killed Duncan a year later in 1040 and took the crown.

Macbeth

Macbeth started his years of rule as the chief of Moray after inheriting the position from his father. He is believed to have been a descendant of Kenneth II of Scotland, while his wife was a descendent of Kenneth III. He had a claim to the Scottish throne when Malcolm II died, but his cousin (Duncan I) inherited it instead due to breaking the customs that were in place about who should get the throne. As a result, conflict broke out between the two factions of the family (Macbeth and his supporters on the one side and Duncan with his supporters on the other).

Macbeth's forces killed Duncan in battle in 1040, following which Macbeth took the throne. There was some warfare with the rebels and nobles during the following years. During the last few years of his reign, Macbeth had to cede parts of southern Scotland to Malcolm III Canmore, the eldest son of Duncan I, due to pressure from opposing forces. Malcolm III proved to be a strong enemy, eventually overcoming and killing Macbeth in battle with the help of the English in 1057. The story of Macbeth's life was formed into a play by Shakespeare, albeit with some alterations from fact.

Lulach

Lulach was the stepson of Macbeth and reigned a period of mere months from 1057 to 1058. His claim came mainly from his mother, who had been a relative of Malcolm II. His uncle was likely the strongest claimant to the throne when Duncan I was put on the throne. His biological father had been the king of Moray, which was a separate kingdom from Scotland at the time. To obtain the crown for Moray, his father had killed Macbeth's father, who had been the reigning Moravian king.

After a short period of exile, Macbeth returned to Moray where he killed Lulach's father and took back the throne that had belonged to his own father. Lulach's mother married Macbeth, and he took Lulach in as his heir. He was thus to inherit both the thrones of Moray and Scotland. Macbeth chose to abdicate in favor of Lulach as he was a younger man who could better handle the threats of Duncan I's sons and their supporters. Lulach was killed in battle a few months into his reign, which paved the way for Malcolm III Canmore to take the throne.

Malcolm III Canmore

After his father had been murdered by MacBeth, Malcolm III remained in exile for more than a decade. He gathered supporters and military forces, killing MacBeth in 1057, after which he took over as ruler. St. Margaret of Scotland was to become his second wife. She was the sister of Edgar Aetheling, who would have been king of England had William the Conqueror's invasion not been so successful.

This was after he had given refuge to Edgar and his sisters while they were in exile from England. Later, Malcolm went on to acknowledge William the Conqueror as the overlord of Scotland in 1072, and Edgar went on to live in France. In the end Malcolm violated the fealty agreement by raiding England multiple times, finally resulting in his death on a raid in 1093. Three of his sons succeeded him on the throne.

Donald Bane

This was the one king who held the throne twice. First, he held it for half a year during 1093 and 1094 and then for three years from later in 1094 to 1097. His brother, Malcolm III, had been king of Scotland for many years. He obtained the crown by laying siege to the castle in Edinburgh and getting elected to the position of king by the lords who were eligible to vote. Duncan II, Malcolm III's son, took the crown with outside support. He had the support of the English, the Normans, and the Saxons.

After having Duncan II killed, Donald retook the throne. The English backed forces to overthrow Donald, which they did successfully after the three years of his second reign. Edgar, a son of Malcolm III, was installed into the position of king after Donald's defeat. With his removal, so went the Celtic customs for electing their king (called tanistry), and a more Norman and Anglo-Saxon style of monarchy was introduced.

Duncan II

Duncan II was the son of Malcolm III who was only on the throne for a few months. He was not accustomed to the Celtic way of life as much as Donald Bane, who was the elected king of Scotland at the time of his assumption of the throne. Growing up as a hostage in the Norman court of England, he was accustomed to the rule of William the Conqueror and was largely under the influence of the new English government. With their backing, he gained the throne, but he wasn't capable of holding the throne in a country where he was essentially a foreigner. Donald Bane and his supporters killed Duncan, allowing Donald to take back the throne.

Sons of Malcolm III Canmore

Edgar, Malcolm III's eldest son, reigned for a decade from 1097 to 1107. Due to his descent from both a Scottish and an English king, he was a uniting force for the Anglo-Saxon and Celtic-descent peoples of the nation. The fealty agreement his father had made to William the Conqueror remained in force, and he was selected to depose his anti-English uncle (Donald Bane) who had taken the throne after his father's death. He was not able to hold the protection Scotland held over the Hebrides from Norwegian raids. As such, he gave the islands to Norway. He left no heir as he had been a devout, unmarried individual, thus leaving the throne to his brother.

His younger brother, Alexander I, reigned over northern Scotland for 17 years from 1107 to 1124. Edgar had specified their younger brother, David I, was to rule over southern Scotland. To keep the peace and honor Scotland's fealty to England, Alexander married an illegitimate daughter (Sibylla) of the English king. Further, he assisted the English king in warfare against Welsh elements, committing to his status as an ally of the English crown. Even though he was an ally of the English and acted in accordance with overlordship, he was committed to keeping the Scottish church independent and under the control of the Scottish monarch.

The youngest of the brothers who reigned (they had three other brothers who didn't rule) was David I. He was the ruler of southern Scotland during the reign of Alexander I, in accordance with their eldest brother's will. When Alexander died, David became the king of the whole of Scotland.

As the king, he was an agent of change. He issued the first Scottish royal coins and established many castles around which some of the most notable Scottish settlements today are located (Edinburgh, Stirling, Roxburgh, and Berwick, among others). Further, he introduced cultural change by bringing in many Anglo-Normans to intermarry and live in Scotland (including the Oliphant, Bruce, Comyn, and Stewart families), so long as those new settlers provided monetary support or military service to the Scottish crown.

He had been present in the English court during the earlier years of his life, thus exposing him to a foreign way of life and Norman sympathies. He married an English noblewoman and went on to hold lands in Huntingdon and Northamptonshire. Part of the reason he succeeded in ruling southern parts of Scotland was because he obtained the help of Normans in England to force his brother Alexander to give him rule in those parts.

The power of David had the effect of influencing the line of succession to the English throne. His recognition of Holy Roman Empress Matilda as heir contributed to her taking the English throne. In order to back her better, he combatted the forces of the man who had been crowned the ruler of England (Stephen) instead of the empress. His support went back and forth between Stephen and Matilda, with the main intention of obtaining more control for himself over Northumberland. Eventually he took power over Northumberland after Matilda's son (whom he had knighted) became the king of England (King Henry II). David remained in power until his death in 1153.

Malcolm IV

King David's firstborn was Malcolm IV, who reigned from 1153 to 1165. He rose to the throne as a child (around age 11), which meant that he didn't have much experience or competence as a ruler. His early death also meant that he couldn't effect much change as an adult, thus putting him at the effect of others' decisions or influence for much of his reign. Before he rose to the position of king of Scotland, however, he had inherited the earldoms of Northumberland and Cumbria, in exchange for the English king's recognition of his earldom of Huntingdon. When he died in his early twenties, the Scottish crown moved to his brother, William I.

William the Lion

William inherited the throne in his early twenties, meaning he was already an adult with full legal capacity at the time. He had also inherited the earldom of Northumberland, which he gave up to the English king in the 1150s—as his older brother did. When he inherited the Scottish throne, William went on the offensive and started attacking the sons of King Henry II of England, the king whom he'd renounced his earldom for. The purpose of the attacks was to gain back the county. Unfortunately, he was captured during a raid he held in 1174 and could only obtain his release by recognizing the English king as overlord of Scotland.

This meant that Scotland was once again under the power of the English king, thereby striking at its independence. Further, the English church was to be recognized as taking superiority over the Scottish church. During the years that followed, William established one of the most affluent abbeys in Scotland.

The years that followed included a lot of back and forth with the church in Rome in an attempt to remove the Church of England as the "middleman." In proceedings with the Pope, William was able to overturn this arrangement in favor of Scotland being under no other churches other than the church in Rome. William was also able to get out of the overlordship arrangement by paying large sums to the English king starting in 1189. The one issue that could not be resolved, however, was that of Northumberland.

The English king forced William to abandon his claim to the county in 1209. This came after years of conflict between the two. Despite the issues of the overlordship, the church, and Northumberland, William had managed to consolidate the power of Scotland into a central authority. The central bureaucracy's officials were able to manage the affairs of the whole nation under the authority and approval of the king. During this period, King William established many of the burghs that are still extant in Scotland. These burghs served to make the central government's work more efficient and effective.

Alexander II

When his father died, Alexander II took over the throne in 1214. His father had been an agent of stability through the process of regaining Scottish dependence with money and getting the church out of the control of the English church. Alexander II took the progress his father had made and built on it by improving relations with England. At first he was on the side of rebel lords who were against the English king John, as he intended to gain English territory for Scotland. However, after John's death and the accession to the throne of Henry III, he both gave public honor to the new king and married his sister to strengthen their ties.

Just over 20 years into the reign of King Henry III, Alexander II signed a peace treaty with him. The effect of the treaty was that Alexander II would have no claim to the English throne, but that he would be granted lands in England. The border between the two nations was set (and is approximately in the same location today). Alexander was concerned not only with the Scottish relations with England but also with interior relations between the crown and the lords of Scotland. He fostered genuine support from lords who had previously only supported the monarchy in formality. Further, he conquered Argyll and brought it under the firm control of the kingdom.

Alexander III

Alexander III had ascended to the throne when he was a boy (in 1249). He had been married to the daughter of the king of England, who was also underage at the time. His father in law wanted to take over control of Scotland to the advantage of himself and England, trying to take control of Alexander III. The result was a political party that advocated for English interests seized the young king. The Scottish took control of the situation by controlling the government under the authority of parties who were against the English. They remained in control until Alexander was of age at 21.

Under Alexander III's reign, the Normans were combatted, and their invasion of Scotland was brought to an end. The Normans already controlled islands off the west coast of Scotland, and they wanted to expand their power to the Scottish mainland. As a result of their defeat, however, the Normans gave control of the Hebrides islands and the Isle of Man to the Scottish. The rule of Alexander III was known to be a period of political and economic stability, with little governing interference from other nations.

His children had all died before him, leaving his granddaughter to inherit the crown after his untimely death in 1286 (he fell off a cliff while riding a horse). The death of his granddaughter before she came of age or had children was the main contributor to the Wars of Scottish Independence.

THE FIRST WAR OF SCOTTISH INDEPENDENCE

King Alexander III had managed the country during a time of relative peace. He had managed to expand the kingdom of the Scots by fostering the Treaty of Perth. As a result of the treaty, Scotland grew to include the Isle of Man and the Outer Hebrides. This happened as the result of warfare between Scotland and the Norwegians, in which the Scottish ultimately gained the winning hand.

Trade was good, and people were able to build up personal wealth. This was about to come to an end. When he died (in 1286), none of his living children remained. His granddaughter, Margaret, was due to inherit the throne after his death. She was the child of his daughter, also named Margaret, and King Eric II of Norway. Unfortunately, she died a mere four years after her grandfather in 1290, leaving Scotland without a leader.

The result was that there were many claimants to the throne. The risk of civil war seemed imminent with factions supporting different claimants. The two largest factions were those who believed the Balliol family should get the crown and those who believed the Bruces should. The king of England (Edward I) was invited to assist in calming the disputes, which he eventually did in 1292 in what is now known as the Great Cause.

Edward eventually decided that John Balliol was to become the Scottish king, but he wanted him to acknowledge Edward's overlordship in return for deciding the matter. John agreed to grant Edward overlordship, but this incited unrest in Scotland. To calm down the situation, John agreed to the Auld Alliance with France in 1295, which served to pacify many of the Scottish. That said, it also had the effect of inciting Edward I to raise an army, which he marched on Scotland in 1296.

Multiple campaigns were led against Edward, such as those of the Scottish Guardians from 1297 to 1304. Another campaign was that of William Wallace, who managed to garner a lot of support, resulting in the success of the Scottish at the Battle of Stirling Bridge. He managed to retain a lot of support until his deciding defeat at the Battle of Falkirk in 1298. All the while, infighting continued throughout Scotland, particularly between the supporters of the Bruce family and the Balliol family.

Robert the Bruce was crowned in 1306, and he campaigned until 1314, gradually driving the English out of the country. In 1314, at the Battle of Bannockburn, the final victory of the First War of Independence was won against the English force of King Edward II. After this, the Scottish started raiding into England itself, and they also helped the Irish in their campaigns against England.

The friction between the two countries gradually reduced, but proper peace was only brought into being after the ratification of the Treaty of Northampton in 1328. Robert Bruce died a year later.

THE GREAT CAUSE: 1292

The predictability of the successor to the crown had ended with the death of Margaret the Maid of Norway when she was eight years old. Her grandfather, King Alexander III, had ruled for almost four decades when he passed. He had three children who would have been eligible for the throne, but all of them passed away before Alexander III died. His only grandchild was Margaret, who was also the daughter of the king of Norway. She was four years old when her grandfather died, thus leaving her as his successor (due to a lack of other living descendants).

This was the cause of confusion, which led to many claimants for the throne. The claimants were members of the greater family tree of the previous kings of Scotland. Many of the claimants had support of powerful individuals and families throughout the nation, thus making for a splintered situation that could have resulted in civil war. A few of the most powerful lords of Scotland, later called the Guardians, asked the king of England (Edward I) to help decide whose claim was the most legitimate. Their intention was to resolve the situation as peacefully as possible.

However, in exchange for Edward's intervention, the Guardians were asked to promise to make him overlord of Scotland. The Guardians stated that they did not have the authority to make such a decision and that he could only discuss such terms with the future king of Scotland once he'd helped with the selection.

Edward thus went ahead to make his selection. He looked at the line of kings who had held the crown over the previous few generations. King David I, who had died in 1153, was the last king to leave surviving descendants. The oldest male descendant was Robert the Bruce's grandfather (who had the same name). The grandfather, however, died in 1295 before any coronation had taken place. The next eldest descendant was John Balliol, who was the son of a Scottish noblewoman and an English nobleman.

Robert the Bruce was younger than John Balliol, thus making John the heir in terms of the law of primogeniture (where the oldest living descendant inherits). To further improve John's claim, the eldest daughter of his common ancestor with Robert was his grandmother, while the second eldest daughter of the common ancestor was Robert's great-grandmother. This meant that John came from the elder existing line of descent of the claims from himself and Robert.

Following the crowing of John, tensions intensified rather than subsided. This was because John's family, who were a powerful family who originated in France and held a lot of property in England, didn't get along with the Scottish nobles and were only eligible for the crown through marriage with Devorgilla, who was a noblewoman whose family held power in Galloway. Thus, the Balliols might have been seen as imposters or as having gotten the crown through luck, whereas the Bruce clan (which Robert was part of) was a powerful and wealthy clan in Scotland (and thus not seen as outsiders). The straw that broke the camel's back was when John accepted Edward I as the overlord of Scotland.

INAUGURATION OF JOHN BALLIOL: 1292

When Edward I selected John Balliol for the throne, he pressured the new king to recognize him as lord paramount of Scotland. This meant that he would be the full title holder of the land of Scotland under feudal law—there would be nobody with a superior title to him over Scotland. John agreed to this, which meant that he would have to provide military support to Edward when told to provide it. This occurred soon after, in 1294 when Edward demanded troops for a war against France.

The Scots people didn't agree with this, and unrest occurred. To pacify them, John agreed to the Auld Alliance, which was ratified as the Treaty of Paris in 1295. Edward retaliated by going to war with Scotland for violating their duties to him as lord paramount of Scotland. This was the start of the Scottish Wars of Independence.

The trading port of Berwick was the first location where the English struck. It was a port of economic value to Scotland. To further incite the Scottish, he took up residence in Berwick Castle for a month.

He then went on a campaign where he struck multiple towns and settlements, including Dunbar, where the

Scottish were subject to a bloodbath. Multiple nobles were captured and sent back to England in captivity in the aftermath of the Battle of Dunbar. Edward rolled on, destroying or taking possession of multiple places, including Jedburgh, Roxburgh, Stirling, and Linlithgow. John Balliol and his nobles submitted to Edward to stop the destructive progression. Edward took John's crown, his royal insignia, the Black Rood of St. Margaret, and the Stone of Destiny. The submission wasn't enough, however, with Edward continuing to pillage and destroy.

AULD ALLIANCE: 1295

The Auld Alliance was the agreement that drew the nations of France and Scotland together. It was ratified in 1295 with the purpose of preventing England's expansion of its borders. The alliance would bring diplomatic and military benefits to both parties, and it would provide the Scots with jobs in the form of being mercenaries for France. It was a valued alliance between the two countries, which brought economic benefits for more than a century.

Likely the most notable use of the alliance was in 1415 after England won a massive victory against France at the Battle of Agincourt. The Scots were asked for aid, in response to which they sent 12,000 troops. The combined troops of France and Scotland beat the English in their first joint battle at the Battle of Baugé in 1421. The Scots troops were rewarded with titles, food, and wine. The next major battle was the Battle of Verneuil in 1424. The forces experienced a heavy loss at the hands of the English, but the cushion of the Scottish soldiers allowed the French enough time to prepare themselves against total domination from the English.

Those Scots that remained in France gained permanent residence. They were able to trade with other Scots back home, with French wine being a particularly hot commodity. A good relationship would continue between the two countries for many centuries. The major turning point for the alliance was after the Scottish Reformation, when the core religion of the two countries differed. The Scottish Reformation also brought a slightly closer relationship between England and Scotland.

WILLIAM WALLACE

In the friction that followed Edward I's enforced recognition as lord paramount of Scotland and raising troops against the Scots for violating that recognition, sentiment grew among the common folk for incitement of a rebellion. William Wallace was one such individual. He killed a sheriff of England and inspired Scottish people to join him as his troops. He managed to gain the support of the Bishop of Glasgow, who lent him enough credibility to gain even more supporters.

Robert the Bruce was one of Edward I's allies at the start of this period of unrest. He was sent by Edward to bring down Wallace and his allies. Robert started carrying out this command, but at the same time started questioning Edward's intentions. He would later change sides and join the rebellion against Edward.

The Battle of Stirling Bridge in 1297 brought a major blow to Edward's campaign of domination. The rebel forces, under the command of Wallace, were able to beat a large English army that was composed largely of cavalry. They did this by allowing the English onto Stirling Bridge, which wasn't very wide, and then pushing back with their spears once there were enough English soldiers on the bridge. With the combination of the narrow bridge, boggy ground, and use of cavalry rather than infantry, the English lost and had to retreat. Wallace was promoted to Guardian of Scotland after this clash.

Skirmishes continued between the sides, but the Battle of Falkirk in 1298 was the major confrontation. The Scots lost this battle and multiple other battles over the next six years. Eventually the Scottish nobles had to submit to Edward, both as a result of atrophied forces and because of infighting among the Bruces and the Balliols (along with their supporters). The submission resulted in the rebellion being outlawed and Wallace becoming a wanted man. When Wallace was captured, Edward directed that he wanted him executed—in return for which he would reduce the intensity of his onslaught.

The execution was gruesome. First, he was pulled to his place of execution by a horse while he was naked. Then he was hung, and his genitals were cut off while he was still alive, only to be burned in front of him. This was followed by being cut open before he died so that his innards could be removed, including his heart. After this, the body was cut into four parts, and his head was chopped off. The parts were sent all over England and Scotland as a display of victory over the leader of the revolutionary forces.

ROBERT THE BRUCE

Robert was from the powerful Bruce clan. His family was related to the royal family of Scotland through marriage. His grandfather had claimed the throne when it was vacant in 1290. His grandfather died before he could rule properly, leaving the throne empty. Using primogeniture (where the oldest living descendant inherits), Edward I awarded John Balliol the crown, not Robert the Bruce. Robert, however, wanted the crown, so he assisted in the insurrection against John Balliol.

Robert remained an ally of Edward I for a few years, but this changed in 1299 when he was made Co-guardian of Scotland with John Comyn. He even assisted William Wallace in his revolts against the English. These two Guardians held a lot of power, both being the head of two of the most influential families of Scotland. The main problem was that the two Guardians didn't get along very well. This came to a head in 1306 when Robert killed John Comyn in Greyfriars Kirk in Dumfries.

Killing him gave Robert the chance he needed to take the position of king as John had been his only real opposition at the time (seeing that Edward I had stripped John Balliol of his crown and royal insignia). However, it also brought renewed vigor in Edward's campaign against Scotland, seeing as John Comyn was married to a cousin of Edward. Nevertheless, Robert was crowned (without Papal approval) and started ruling the Scots.

REIGN AS KING: 1306–1314

The English tried to quash Robert and his forces, with Robert experiencing two big defeats during his first half year as king. The aftermath of the defeat included executions of his siblings, the imprisonment of his wife, and going on the run (out of Scotland) to escape Scottish allies of England. Legend says watching a spider spin a web gave him the inspiration he needed to be patient and have hope for success. Upon this inspiration, he traveled to the south of Scotland in 1307 to garner support and win minor victories.

The minor victories helped him gain more supporters. The death of Edward I in 1307 helped him gain even more supporters as Edward II wasn't yet as experienced an opponent as his father. The rebel forces thus gained traction and started pushing the English out of Scotland over the next few years. The final victory came at the Battle of Bannockburn in 1314.

Battle of Bannockburn: 1314

The Battle of Bannockburn took place in 1314 when the Scottish had overcome all the English strongholds in Scotland other than the castle at Stirling. Edward II had assembled large forces at the castle with the intention of protecting the interests of all those loyal to him in Scotland. While Robert had a lower number of forces, his troops laid proper groundworks, and they used the surrounding forest tactically.

Once the battle started, there was some back and forth between the forces. It seemed like the Scots were retreating after a seeming stalemate between the forces. This wasn't the case because the Scots were merely altering their position to cut off the English forces. In the clash that followed, Robert and an English night faced each other in personal combat for most members of both armies to see. Robert cut off the knight's head, after which the English troops retreated.

That night the Scots were in a celebratory mood, while the English had a rough night. The following day the Scots started off with prayer and a religious service, followed by meeting the English troops in battle. The earthworks they laid proved to be disastrous for the English, and the Scots eventually won. Edward II fled with his life.

In the aftermath of the battle, the Scots considered that they had won their freedom from overlordship. This, however, wasn't formalized until 14 years later with the signing of the Treaty of Northampton.

Declaration of Arbroath: 1320

In the 1290s, the Pope directed the Scots to seek a peace agreement with the English. This wasn't done as the Scots wanted to break out of the yoke of the English king. When Robert the Bruce incited further rebellion, this went directly against the Pope's direction. Then in 1306, when he killed John Comyn, the murder took place in Greyfriars Kirk, thus violating the laws of the church. Robert confessed to the crime, and the Bishop of Glasgow absolved him. Despite this, Edward I outlawed Robert, and the Pope excommunicated him.

The excommunication was ignored, and Robert was crowned by Scottish bishops a month after the murder. The bishops went against the excommunication with the intention of advocating for the autonomy of Scotland. Thus, while he was crowned, the coronation wasn't sanctioned by the Pope and would not be recognized by all internationally. A letter of excommunication was resent in 1308.

When they were invited to the Council of Vienne in 1310, the Scottish clergy requested that the Pope recognize Robert as king. They wanted him to absolve Robert of the murder that took place in Greyfriars Kirk. Absolution was granted, but not by the Pope, rather by a cardinal. The absolution letter granted him absolution for the murder, but didn't grant him approval to be king. In fact, the letter referred to him as a layman.

The Scottish nobles wanted to receive proper recognition for their independence and their king. They sent the Declaration of Arbroath to the Pope with this intention. The declaration was given the seal of 8 earls and 40 barons of Scotland. The letter showed a unification in the nobles of Scotland and indicated that all they wanted was freedom as a nation.

As a result of the declaration, the Pope sent a letter to Edward II stating that he wanted Edward to make peace with the Scots. Further, Robert was recognized by the Pope as lawful king of Scotland in 1324. Eventually the English caved and recognized Scotland's independence in 1328.

The Last Years of His Reign

Edward II was deposed in 1327. His successor was Edward III, but a regent was put in place until the boy king could take on full responsibility for daily affairs. The regent wanted to maintain peace with the Scots, resulting in the Treaty of Northampton in 1328. This was partly with the intention of reducing the amount of raids that the Scottish had continually been taking into the north of England since the success at the Battle of Bannockburn in 1314. The kingdom of Scotland itself had been relatively free of infighting over the last decade of Robert's reign, largely with him being perceived as the uniting figure of the nation who had overcome the English.

THE TREATY OF NORTHAMPTON: 1328

This treaty brought final peace between the two nations since the start of conflict with Edward I in the 1290s. The treaty stated that the English agreed that the Scottish could govern themselves under their own king and that Robert I (the formal title for Robert the Bruce) was acknowledged as rightfully holding the crown. The treaty further agreed that the kings and their nations would be allies that would provide each other with mutual assistance.

Further, provisions were made to take the Auld Alliance into account. If the Scots were to assist the French in warfare against the English, then the English would be allowed to retaliate against the Scottish. In exchange for the concessions from England, the Scottish would have to pay a large sum of silver. They would also have to conclude a marriage contract between the son of Robert the Bruce and the sister of Edward III.

In the next chapter, we will look at the reign of the Stewart monarchs of Scotland. This will start with the reign of David II, the last non-Stewart monarch, so as to provide context. The Second War of Scottish Independence, the Scottish Renaissance, and the Scottish Reformation will also be included as major events immediately preceding or happening during the Stewart line's reign.

CHAPTER 3
THE REIGN OF THE STEWART KINGS

The Stewart monarchs descended from Robert the Bruce. His daughter had married a man called Walter the Steward, hence the surname Stewart. Their reign over Scotland spanned through the Late Middle Ages, the Renaissance, and the unification with England. In this chapter we will explore their reigns and important developments that took place during these times.

THE SECOND WAR OF INDEPENDENCE

The Second War of Scottish Independence started in 1332—four years after signing the Treaty of Northampton. The instigation of this was likely resumption of the conflict between the Bruce and Balliol factions for the throne when Robert the Bruce died. The four-year-old David II (Robert's son) was the selected successor, but his guardian died while he was young, and he was married to the sister of Edward III, which complicated matters. Further, the Balliols were disinherited by Robert the Bruce, inciting them and those loyal to them to join with Edward III in an attempt to take the crown.

The Battle of Mar, which was part of the ensuing conflict, resulted in the death of the lord of Mar, who was the regent of David II. The lord of Liddesdale, who was an illegitimate son of Robert the Bruce, was also killed in battle. This left no protection for the young king, resulting in Edward Balliol (son of John Balliol) being crowned a few weeks later. He ruled over some parts of Scotland while David II was growing up, with his chief point of operations being in Galloway.

David II was sent to be cared for by the king of France, Philip VI, in 1334 to keep him safe. Control of the parts of Scotland that weren't under the control of Edward Balliol was handed over to the newly chosen Guardians of the kingdom. The unrest between the Balliol and Bruce factions continued, with neither party gaining full control of the kingdom. David returned to Scotland in 1341, at the age of 17.

Edward III resumed warfare with France in 1346, at which point the king of France asked Scotland for aid in return for acting as guardian to David II and also in line with the Auld Alliance. The Scots thus invaded England, while the English invaded France. English forces met the Scots at the Battle of Neville's Cross, in which David II was captured and a former regent, the earl of Moray, was killed. David was imprisoned in London for 12 years, and he wasn't allowed to contact any of his citizens from Scotland. Eventually a truce was concluded under the Treaty of Berwick, which allowed David to be released in return for a large ransom. The treaty signaled the end of the Second War of Scottish Independence.

EARLY STEWART KINGS

To gain context, we will look at the last non-Stewart king of Scotland (David II), including the entwined reign of Edward Balliol. This will be followed by the Stewart kings up to the reign of Mary, Queen of Scots.

DAVID II

The period during which David II ruled was a turbulent one. When his father died, he was just a child, and Edward Balliol (John Balliol's son) was given the throne by the English. He was the de facto ruler of Scotland while David II grew up, with the lords of Scotland splintering and the sense of unity under Robert the Bruce being lost.

Edward obtained the crown by invading Scotland with a French army, getting the backing of English lords who had their Scottish lands removed during the reign of Robert the Bruce. As such, he started off his reign by undoing a lot of the unification that had taken place over the previous decades. First, Edward ruled for three months, but he was forced out later in the year of his inauguration (1332). The English king had assisted in getting Edward back on the throne to continue his rule, for which Edward gave away parts of southern Scotland.

He took it back the following year, but did so after agreeing that the king of England was to be the overlord of Scotland. This struck back at the independence that had been fought for during his predecessor's reign. He had a lot of ties to the French and English, having spent much of his earlier life there. Thus, his loyalties were not necessarily with his own people. He ended up giving all his Scottish lands and titles to the English king, thus striking hard against the independence of Scotland.

David II was a much better liked candidate for the throne by the Scottish people as his father had brought a lot of the country together. Further, David II had more loyalties to the Scottish than the English or French, being from a prominent clan that had established themselves in the region over the previous two centuries. His main connection with England was the marriage that had taken place between him and the sister of Edward III of England (he was four at the time and she was seven). That said, the marriage was arranged as part of the terms of the Treaty of Northampton, and David wasn't raised in England or with English guardians.

David II would have taken the throne as a boy, but the forces of the English king were too powerful, and his regent had to throw in the towel. David II thus went into exile and grew up in the court of the French king (as his descendant Mary, Queen of Scots, would 200 years later). As his teenage years came to a close, he assisted in fighting battles with the French against the English. He was able to enter Scotland and gain his authority of king in multiple regions in 1341.

While on the throne, his attention remained preoccupied with fighting his English counterpart. In one of these conflicts, David II was injured and taken prisoner. The English let him go, on the condition that Scotland would pay a large fee for his release. The fee was too much, so David II agreed that the son of the English king would take the Scottish throne when he died (which happened in 1371). This agreement, combined with a closer friendship with the English king and financial wastefulness, served to alienate his kingdom from him. Parliament took control and voted against the agreement he'd made with the English regarding his succession, giving the crown to his nephew Robert II instead.

ROBERT II

Robert II was already old when he took the throne, or at least by the standards of the time (age 55). He had some experience with power when he took the throne in 1372 due to his prior position as earl of Strathearn. He was the first Stewart king, with Walter the Steward being his father. With the assistance of Parliament, he took control of the situation when David II tried to make the English king's son his heir in exchange for canceling his outstanding ransom payments. As a result, Scotland's relationship with England deteriorated, and war broke out again four years after Robert II's reign started. He didn't make any large reforms or bring major improvements during his rule.

During the last few years of his period as king, his sons administered the nation on his behalf. Robert II's sex life contributed to later stability of the kingdom. He had nine children from his first wife (with their marriage taking place after the births), thus giving rise to questions about their legitimacy. He also had eight illegitimate sons (that we know of). His second marriage produced four legitimate children, but strife ensued between them and the children from his first marriage—some of his first wife's children feeling they should have been eligible for the crown. His reign ended with his death in 1390.

ROBERT III

A child from his father's first marriage, Robert III was the regent of Scotland during the four of the later years of his father's reign (1384–1388) due to his father's old age. In 1388 he was injured, leaving him incapable of effectively holding power until his death in 1406. Nevertheless, he was crowned king in 1390 when his father died. Almost all of his reign was governed by regents.

Robert Stewart, First Duke of Albany

The third son of Robert II and a brother to Robert III, Robert Stewart was never formally crowned the king of Scotland. That said, he was the regent of Scotland for the last two years of his father's life (1388–1390) and for the first eight years of his brother's reign (1390–1398), after which the eldest son of Robert III took over the role of regent. When the son started being too much at odds with Robert

Stewart, he was locked up and eventually died, paving the way for Robert Stewart to be chosen to resume the position of regent after the death of Robert III in 1406.

The new king, James I, was unable to govern due to being held prisoner in London. Despite the king being held by the English, Robert Stewart continued waging war with them. He held the position of regent until his death in 1420, most of which time the main priority was warring with the English. His son took over both his dukedom and the regency, but lasted only five years before being executed on the commands of James I.

THE RENAISSANCE IN SCOTLAND

The Scottish Renaissance started later than in many other countries. It started in the fifteenth century with the advent of the printing press as an instigator. The printing press allowed literature to be spread around more freely, and it encouraged the use of the written word in everyday life. This section will look at the major aspects of the Renaissance and the effect it had.

POLITICS

The royal court was the instigator of the social revolution that took place during the Scottish Renaissance. It brought ideas of sophistication and reform from foreign nations due to the intermarriage that took place between the French and English royal families, among other non-royal families of money and influence. James IV was perhaps the most influential royal proponent for the Renaissance. He was an advocate for better education and improved literacy, both in Latin and in the vernacular of Scotland.

Use of Latin improved the population's interchange of ideas with the continent. People of the continent used Latin as their lingua franca at the time. Use of the Scottish written language also meant that classical literature and the history of Scotland could be disseminated better to the common masses. The introduction and support for the use of the printing press were a contributor to this exchange of ideas and the elevation of the population's literacy, especially since it ensured that written language wasn't something only available to the wealthy or those working for the church.

A prominent political idea that spread as a result of the increased literacy and interchange of ideas was that the ruler had to rule for the well-being of the commoners, not just their own interests. During this period, Parliament of Scotland gained traction, resulting in seniority being given to the law over the king. The advance in demand for a more active government resulted in a permanent navy and armed force to protect the people and taxes becoming more orderly.

RELIGION

Exposure to Protestant ideas was one of the effects of the Renaissance. Restructuring of the church was taking place in many countries on the continent, as well as England. The printing press also meant that Bibles were easier to obtain, resulting in people being able to gain its knowledge for themselves, rather than through someone else's interpretation. Faith became more important to the Scots, and they could better emulate what was written by gaining a personal understanding. People were also exposed to other fields like theology, philosophy, and science. They could thus gain alternate perspectives that either altered or enhanced their religious beliefs.

OTHER DEVELOPMENTS

Development of the arts was one of the main outcomes of the Renaissance. Painting and crafts took on new knowledge, as well as literature and architecture. The manners a person used to conduct themselves started showing their level of sophistication. Further, displays of power became more important as people cared more about the impression they gave others. This contributed to bringing about a social revolution.

The social revolution placed more value on personal usefulness than before. In earlier times, people's families and their connections were everything. However, with the Renaissance, the desirable skills and knowledge someone held would determine the amount of wealth they could amass.

Even the royal family's status shifted from their right to rule to their capacity to hold the ruling position. While their position had elevated because of the Renaissance, the use of mathematics to get better weapons was of more importance. The royals were able to amass better weapons to protect themselves, thus making it much more difficult for other nobles to try to overcome them. The shift was thus from connections to capacity to hold their own.

KINGS OF THE RENAISSANCE

JAMES I

James was the king of Scotland from 1406 until his death in 1437. That said, he only assumed the role of king in 1424 due to being held prisoner for more than a decade in London (from the very start of his reign). Despite being unable to govern directly for his first years as king, he still managed to get his uncle (Robert Stewart) imprisoned and later (likely as a result of his orders) executed in 1420. The years from 1420 to 1424 were ruled by a regency of Robert Stewart's son, until the king of England released James in that final year. During James's reign, control was taken of the war with England, and the priority became governing Scotland and its people.

He started his period of direct reign by having multiple lords, including the son of Robert Stewart, taken into custody. Some of them were executed for crimes such as treason. Relations with the Highland lords were also strengthened, with attempts made at improving their loyalty to the crown. He was a well-educated man who wrote a long poetry book, The King's Book.

He was driven in cleaning out the governing system of the country. Financial matters in the kingdom were brought under his direct supervision. There was a crackdown on bribery and corruption. Payments from the church to Rome were reduced in an attempt to bolster the nation's financial wealth. There was also a push to improve the administration of justice to the common people. When he was assassinated in 1437, his assassin and conspirators were captured and executed on the orders of his widow (Joan Beaufort).

JAMES II

The start of his reign was turbulent. He was inaugurated at the age of six when his dad passed away. The kingdom grew in instability because families of power tried to gain control of the regency and raising of the adolescent king. Some of the advancements that James I brought fell away due to the friction between the factions, thereby taking away focus from the common people and governing.

James II officially took over his duties in 1449 at the age of 19. As his father had done, he confiscated the property of lords who had caused trouble for the monarchy. He used their lands to generate income to fund various expenses and campaigns of the kingdom. The main reforms he made were to re-establish the central government and improve administration of justice through all strata of society.

England once again started asserting that it had the authority to rule Scotland. Conflict thus resumed more substantially with England, with multiple raids being made by James II and his forces. He died in a siege in 1460.

JAMES III

James III ruled for 28 years from 1460 to 1488, starting at the age of eight. The first six years of his reign were ruled by regents, including his mother. He was kidnapped after this (age 14) by a collection of Scottish lords. These lords effectively took control of his upbringing and ruling of the country for the next three years.

The rest of his reign after he took back control from the lords wasn't any less tumultuous. The problem was partly that he was out of touch with many of his nobles by championing the arts and being less driven by their interests or concerns. Things got worse.

He arrested two of his brothers on suspicion of treason. The one brother, the duke of Albany, was able to escape and fled to England. Meanwhile, James III had confiscated both brothers' lands and property. The duke of Albany enlisted the help of English armed forces to march back to Scotland and demand back his lands. They were successful in pressuring the king to do so, but the king managed to push his brother back out a year later.

Many of the nobles were alienated during this period, resulting in them jumping on the bandwagon when the English soldiers entered the country. They tried to rebel against the king, which he was able to quash on multiple occasions. During the rebellions, some of James III's best supporters were killed by the rebels, resulting in reduced support for the king. In the end the revolts proved to be successful. James III's son and successor was won over to the cause of the rebels, and James III himself was killed after being captured in 1488.

JAMES IV

James IV was a king who was actively involved in the internal affairs of Scotland. He reigned from the age of 15 in 1488 until his death while fighting on foot in the Battle of Flodden in 1513. When the nobles of Scotland rose up against his father in rebellion, James IV sympathized with their concerns. This would be shown during his reign.

His inauguration after the death of his father was followed by five years of actively interacting with the lords of Scotland. He did not only try to build relations with those in the south but pursue stronger relations with those in the Highlands as well. All the lords of Scotland were brought under his authority in one way or another, including conquest.

When James IV had the whole kingdom under his control, he focused on upgrading the power of the central government. Financial matters of the kingdom were included in this new central authority. The royal household was brought to a high standard of education and refinement, and political discourse was elevated. The result was that the finances of Scotland were improved and the nation started being seen as a refined one among the other powers of the continent.

He was a champion of the arts and learning. This was quite appropriate for the time as the Renaissance had been taking the world by storm for more than a century. The nation itself had entered the Renaissance during the reign of his father, and the concepts of artistic, political, and economic improvements were relevant issues of the day. In line with this, Janes IV vigorously supported improvements in education, the introduction of printing presses to Scotland, and patronage of art (specifically literature).

The relationship between Scotland and England was to become an issue during the seventh year of James IV's reign. He had supported a pretender to the English throne, resulting in breakage of a brief period of calm between the nations. As a result, conflict broke out between the nations. Multiple invasions and raids took place.

The situation was pacified when James IV married Margaret Tudor, the eldest daughter of the new English king (Henry VII). He had his successor and only legitimate child with Margaret (although he had many illegitimate children too). A peace agreement was brought into place as a result of their marriage, relationship, and successors.

The behavior that dishonored the agreement was continued skirmishes and raids across the mutual border of the nations. These skirmishes didn't cause serious national problems, but things would change when Henry VIII took power in England. Friction between the two nations was largely due to mounting tension between France and England. Scotland was a major ally of France and backed it in the warfare that would follow between France, England, and other European nations.

The end came soon after England invaded France. While the English forces were occupied with the French, the Scottish troops invaded England. Multiple raids were carried out, but James IV would die in the process. At the Battle of Flodden in Northumberland, he died while fighting on foot, leaving the kingdom to his son with Margaret Tudor.

Margaret Tudor

Margaret married James IV when she was 14 years old in 1489. She was the oldest daughter of the English king Henry VII. Henry VIII was her little brother. While her husband was alive, she was loyal to Scotland and its interests. And when he died, she took over the regency for her son, the infant king James V.

Her behavior during this time would contribute to military and political difficulties later on. She would shift her allegiances back and forth between France and England, largely dependent on her financial interests. While she was a daughter to an English monarch, her loyalty wasn't necessarily very strong as her father had provided a small dowry when she married James IV.

She married Archibald Douglas, a pro-English man, the year after James IV's death. Parliament didn't look kindly on her quick remarriage, and they also didn't approve of her shifting back and forth between her allegiances. They replaced her as the regent and sent her into exile. She lived her exile out in England, during which time she and her husband became estranged. As such, she had their marriage annulled to allow her to remarry in 1527.

Her third husband was Henry Stewart, who would go on to have a beneficial relationship with his stepson, King James V. James V had taken the role of king directly into his hands by that time. He made his stepfather Lord Malvern and took both him and Margaret on as two of his closest advisors. The relationship of advisors continued for many years until it was discovered that Margaret was betraying both her country and her son.

She had been sending confidential information to her brother, King Henry VIII, in England. Betrayal of state secrets was a major crime, as it is today. As such, James sent her away so that she couldn't participate in political affairs. She remained out of the political sphere until her death in 1541.

JAMES V

He came into power when he was less than a year old in 1513. During his first year, his mother served as his regent. This was followed by John Stewart, the duke of Albany, serving as his regent from 1514 to 1524. His mother was his regent once more from 1524 to 1525. His stepfather, Archibald Douglas, imprisoned the young king from 1526 to 1528 after a brief period of guardianship had lapsed. He did this with the intention of consolidating power for his own benefit.

James escaped the imprisonment and forced Archibald to flee to England. He then took on rule directly, starting with consolidation of the kingdom under his central authority. In 1534 he ratified the Treaty of Perpetual Peace with Henry VIII of England, which had the intention of bringing a truce between the two countries. Four years later he married Mary of Lorraine (also called Mary de Guise), who was a noblewoman from a noble family.

The last few years of his reign, James became more demanding with his taxes. He was strict regarding religious devotion and showed himself to be a harsh individual. In 1542, Henry VIII attacked Scotland, and his nobles didn't support his army. They despised his cruelty and weren't willing to respond to his call to arms, resulting in an easy victory for Henry VIII. He had a mental breakdown and died later that year. His daughter, Mary, Queen of Scots, was born six days after his death.

THE REFORMATION IN SCOTLAND

The writings of Martin Luther regarding religious reform started appearing in the 1520s. They didn't gain much traction with the Scots at first because they were a devout Catholic nation and the effects of the Renaissance were only just starting to show. The "Act anent heresy" was passed in 1525, which stated that anyone caught importing or reading the ideas about religious reform would have to forfeit their possessions. This gave Scots even less motivation to alter their behavior.

Things started changing in the late 1520s. Patrick Hamilton, a student who returned from Germany in 1527, started sharing Lutheran ideas. He was burned at St. Salvador's College in 1528, drawing public attention to what was going on.

The small number of people who had started converting to Protestantism now had a martyr to advocate for their stance. They vandalized multiple Catholic buildings from 1528 to 1532, drawing more attention to their message. Another student with Protestant beliefs was tried and executed in 1533 at St. Salvador's College, giving another martyr for the cause. Further executions were performed at the college in 1538 and 1539, drawing more attention.

The seeming reign of terror of James V resulted in more questioning the status quo of the church and the monarchy. To cool the flames of violence, Mary de Guise took on a tolerant frame of mind toward new religious persuasions. She advocated for Catholicism but didn't fully stop people from exploring the ideas of Protestantism. The attempts at bringing unity between England and Scotland during the early 1540s would have negated an open anti-Protestant policy framework. That said, she didn't try to bring about a better understanding between the religious factions or try to understand her Protestant nobles' perspectives better.

When commitments were renewed with France after moving Mary, Queen of Scots, to live with the French king in 1548, a firmer stance was necessitated. The French were an intensely Catholic country, and their royal family swayed Mary de Guise to take a more anti-Protestant perspective. Further, Mary Tudor was instituted as the queen of England in 1553, which briefly put a Catholic ruler on their throne. This meant that Protestants in Scotland couldn't cross the border to live in a more tolerant country. Tensions rose, and skirmishes became more common. While England reverted to a Protestant country in 1558 under Elizabeth I, this couldn't revert the tension that had been formed in Scotland over the previous five years.

Rebellion broke out in Scotland during 1559. The rebellion started when Mary de Guise took control of Perth. Once it was under her control, she imposed martial law and exacted the Catholic way of worship on its citizens. A boy was killed by her troops in this process, providing a show of brutality that the common people and the Protestants could unite behind against the regent. Further, James Stewart (illegitimate son of James V) retaliated by declaring for the reformers.

Once he declared for them, he conquered both Fife and Edinburgh with the intention of bringing religious change. With his allies, the Lords of the Congregation, Protestant power was exerted in multiple parts of Scotland. Further, Parliament outlawed Catholicism in 1560 and renounced both the legal power and spiritual custodianship of the Pope over the kingdom.

A group of Protestant ministers worked out a series of reforms for the churches of Scotland starting in 1561. John Knox was included among their ranks. When Mary, Queen of Scots, returned to Scotland in the same year (after her mother, Mary de Guise, had died), she walked into a highly conflicted environment. She had been brought up Catholic in France and wished to continue practicing her faith accordingly. That said, she didn't want to upset the powerful Protestant powers of the nation. As such, she worked with her half brother, James Stewart, to create a more religiously tolerant policy for Scotland.

With the turmoil at the end of Mary's reign, largely due to smear campaigns about her love life, she wasn't able to hold onto her power any longer. Her half brother thus took over as regent for her son, James VI, who was crowned after her deposition. He was brought up Protestant, with James Buchanan (of radical Calvinist affiliation) being one of his main tutors. Protestantism had become the common religion of Scotland by the time he started ruling directly. He continued James Stewart's pro-Protestant approach and perhaps took it even further.

He contributed to the reform of the Kirk (the Church of Scotland) by introducing the Episcopacy. This meant that he would choose who would hold the position of bishop. The bishops he chose would then go ahead to govern the church, thus making him their formal leader. He also used the development of the printing press to introduce cheaper Bibles so that almost everyone could get their own copy. Training of ministers was a priority, with him opening the University of Edinburgh to cater to the new demand for a large body of educated Protestant clergy.

He introduced a catechism of questions for churchgoers and ballads that were formed into church songs. Courts of church elders were formed, with the intention of disciplining their congregations. Congregations were expected to behave in a manner that was deemed appropriate and to attend church services regularly. They investigated matters under their jurisdiction, such as sexual offenses, and meted out disciplinary measures to counteract behavior that wasn't appropriate to their codes. With these changes, the Reformation came to an end, and the practice of belief was altered permanently in both England and Scotland.

JOHN KNOX

John Knox was likely the most well-known proponent of the Scottish Reformation. He was born in 1514 to a family that had little money. He was dissatisfied with the way society was structured and wanted change. The Catholic church was seen as an institution that had built up a position of power and affluence, partly through corruption (mainly from bribery), yet not providing enough care to adherents in need. Morals were seen as lacking in the Catholic church, and the most important clergy were often foreign.

John approved of the writings of early Protestant authors and later grew to become an ardent supporter of John Calvin. He had many Protestant friends from a young age, with more than one of them being executed for heresy due to their beliefs. This further built on his opinion of the Catholic church being made up of persecutors. His views extended to Mary de Guise and other powerful people whom he saw as capable of making change yet weren't willing to.

While in exile in England, he experienced the Protestant reign of Edward VI. He had a high opinion of the young king and became his royal chaplain. Knox contributed to writing the English book of common prayer. The young king passed away before the prayer book could be issued, and his successor was the Catholic queen Mary Tudor. He criticized the new queen and her religious morality, including finding fault because she was a woman in a position of ruling.

When Elizabeth I was instated, however, the prayer book was published, and she reinstituted Protestantism. He returned to Scotland soon after Elizabeth I's reign started and just before Mary, Queen of Scots, came back from France.

He fought to establish a reformed Protestant church and worked closely with James Stewart and his allies. When Mary, Queen of Scots, returned in 1561, he criticized her reign from the very beginning, largely because of her Catholic affiliation. Gradually the Protestant elements of Scotland gained power, while Mary and the Catholic elements lost theirs. When she was in England after her deposition, Protestantism was made the official religion of Scotland. John died five years after Mary's son, James VI, was born. Before he died, however, he played a part in teaching the boy to take on a Protestant outlook in life (seeing as the boy had been baptized a Roman Catholic).

MARY, QUEEN OF SCOTS

Mary, Queen of Scots, was born in 1542. Multiple persons of power (including Henry VIII) wanted to take control of her upbringing to both influence her outlooks in life and have the power of regent. Her mother ultimately won and was her first regent. At age five, Mary was sent to France to be brought up in the care of the king of France. Mary's mother was of the Valois and Guise families (both being families of money and power in France), which influenced her decision to send the young queen abroad.

Her life in the court of the French king was sheltered, with many luxuries and a good education made available. For all intents and purposes, she had become a French woman and lost touch with her Scottish identity—even her first language was French. She married Francis II of France a year before he became king of France in 1559, but he died a year later due to an ear condition. She thus returned to Scotland in 1561, after both her husband and mother had died.

Upon her return, the situation of the Protestant and Catholic conflict demanded most of her attention. Further, Francis II's father had claimed the English throne on her behalf when she was a girl, resulting in Elizabeth I having a hostile attitude toward Mary from the start. Mary was a threat to Elizabeth's rule. There was thus tension both locally and with Scotland's more powerful southern neighbor. To pacify the situation, she adopted a position of religious tolerance with the help of her half brother, James Stewart (who was a Protestant noble).

Four years after her return (1565), Mary married Henry Stewart, Lord Darnley. This poured fuel on the fire because he was disliked by many nobles in the Scottish court. Further, due to both him and Mary being Stewarts (also Stuarts), this made the couple more of a threat to Elizabeth I's rule than they had been individually. James Stewart, who had been one of her closest advisors, was also antipathetic to her new husband.

The year after her marriage (1566), both Lord Darnley and James Stewart were involved in a plot to remove Mary from the throne, along with multiple other nobles. She was heavily pregnant at the time. The first step was to kill David Riccio, one of her confidants and friends, in front of Mary. Lord Darnley withdrew from the plot before it came into fruition, likely because of getting ill and because Mary had given birth to their heir. He died in 1567 after an explosion at his home outside of Edinburgh—with strangulation marks being found around his neck.

Those with vested interests against her started sharing the idea that Mary was responsible for Lord Darnley's death. They stated that she had plotted his death with James Hepburn, the fourth earl of Bothwell. She was further accused of having had an affair with Bothwell at the time of the alleged plotting. When Mary married Bothwell three months after Lord Darnley's death, it lent credence to the accusations, and factions that were against her managed to get her deposed. Her one-year-old son was crowned as her replacement.

After the deposition she was kept under house arrest, which she escaped in 1468 in an attempt to reclaim her throne. This didn't go as planned, so she fled to England soon after to seek refuge with Elizabeth I. Due to Mary's earlier claims to the English throne and factions who were against Elizabeth, she imprisoned Mary to keep her throne safe. The imprisonment lasted for 18 years, during which time Mary wrote requests to be relieved many times. Eventually Mary resorted to conspiring an escape.

The conspiracy involved the remaining Catholic individuals of power in England trying to get her to take the throne. It involved the death of Elizabeth I. Mary might not have been an active conspirator in all of the plan, but the risk the plan posed when discovered gave Elizabeth no choice but to have Mary tried for treason. Mary was tried in an English court of law, which sentenced her to death by beheading in 1587.

With Mary dead and James VI in power, the Stewart line took on not only the Scottish throne but also the English throne. The following period resulted in the union of the crowns and the union of Parliaments. The next chapter will cover the unions and the concurrent Jacobite risings.

CHAPTER 4
THE UNION OF THE CROWNS AND THE UNION OF PARLIAMENTS

Scotland had been a nation holding power in the north of Great Britain for more than a thousand years. Although there had been many attempts to conquer it, none permanently succeeded. In the end, it was the Scots who subjugated their neighbors on the island through the unification of the crowns under James VI.

JAMES VI

James VI was the son of Mary, Queen of Scots, and Lord Darnley. He was born in 1566 and crowned as king in 1567. A range of tutors were used to raise him as his father was dead and his mother was imprisoned for most of his life. Four regents ruled on his behalf before he took direct control of the throne. He took direct control after he was captured in 1582 (age 15) in a plot to place his mother back on the throne, after which he gradually took more control of issuing his own policies.

He pursued an alliance with England in 1585, both in an attempt to ensure peaceful relations between the countries and in an attempt to be nominated by Elizabeth I as her heir.

The English were a Protestant nation, which made them a better ally for Scotland as a country with a new bulk of Protestant citizens than the long-term ally that was France (seeing that France was strictly Catholic). When his mother was executed in 1587, he didn't provide any strong protest, but rather prioritized the relationship he'd been maintaining with Elizabeth.

He remained largely uninvolved in the affairs of his Protestant and Catholic nobles, allowing them to exhaust their resources against each other so that he could retain absolute rule without opposition. He believed that he was entitled to his rule by God and declared himself to be the head of the Presbyterian Church of Scotland. When Elizabeth I eventually died without children in 1603, he was named her heir. He was a valid claimant, both due to his line of descent and his faith.

When he took on the English crown, both England and Scotland had a joint ruler. This was called the union of the crowns, and James later stylized himself as being the king of Great Britain. He moved to London and had the affairs of Scotland run through a privy council in his name. He corresponded with them using letters to keep abreast of the happenings of the kingdom. He also had a royal commissioner who represented him at the Scottish Parliament.

While he managed to hold onto the affairs of Scotland without too much trouble, he faced a lot of difficulties as the king of England. He was known to be extravagant and wasn't capable of resolving the debt that had been accrued by England during the wars with Spain under Elizabeth I. He also had multiple disagreements with the English Parliament, partly due to employing multiple poorly chosen advisors. There was also the factor that he didn't understand the English people as well on a cultural level. He couldn't remedy this very easily because the English monarch was expected to remain more distant from the common citizens than the Scottish.

During the last year before his death in 1625, his son and heir, Charlies I, and the duke of Buckingham administered his kingship on his behalf. He had become old and didn't have the necessary capacity to wield the power needed to administer the countries under his dominion (England, Ireland, Scotland, and the colonies).

THE UNION OF THE CROWNS

When James VI inherited the English crown in 1603, the union of the crowns took place. The crowns of Scotland and England had never before been held by the same person. He soon stylized himself the king of Great Britain and had the Union Jack created from a combination of St. George's Cross and the Cross of St. Andrew. He tried to convince the English Parliament to remove anti-Scottish legislation and to install pro-Scottish laws, which succeeded on a superficial level. The English Parliament agreed to repeal the most hostile of laws against the Scots.

During this time, the laws of both countries were their own, and they each had their own Parliament (until the Acts of Union in 1707). The economy of each country was completely separate, along with their churches. That said, the same ruler dictated what was to be done in the government of both countries. Further, the conduct of both governments was to be carried out in such a way that it didn't have too heavy a detrimental effect on England.

The effect on the Scottish economy was an overall negative one during the first century after the union. France and the Netherlands were two of Scotland's best long-term trading partners. When they went to war with England, Scotland was prevented from backing them, which resulted in embargoes from those countries against Scotland. Religious affairs of Scotland also received a blow. Gradual changes were implemented that aligned the Scottish Kirk with the structure of the Church of England.

The biggest effect, however, was the absence of James VI (and following monarchs) from Scotland on a physical level. This came to a head with James VI's successor, Charles

I. The Scots felt like they had no monarch present and caring for or guiding them, while the English felt that they were being led by a foreign king who didn't understand them.

CHARLES I

Charles I grew up in Scotland while his family moved to England. He was a shy child who stammered. His manners and temper were both good, and he had no known vices. However, he was out of touch with his citizens because he only mixed with the upper classes and he didn't travel much. As an individual living in a near-ivory tower, his method of connecting with the world was through art and religion.

In 1625, at the age of 25, he inherited the role of king. He believed that God had given him the absolute right to rule. This was a problem in England where Parliament had gained a lot of power in the recent past. Frequent clashes occurred between the king and Parliament throughout his rule, mainly over matters relating to taxation. He was known to dissolve Parliament on more than one occasion. At one point he thought that Parliament was taking on a revolutionary tone, after which he refused to call a new Parliament for 11 years (from 1629 to 1640) and imposed his personal rule on the country.

He had alienated himself from his Scottish nobles by enforcing practices of the Anglican church on them (by introducing a new liturgy and ecclesiastical policy). An assembly of ministers and prominent members of the public took place in Glasgow in 1638, resulting in the National Covenant. This cut off much of Charles's power over the Kirk.

The Bishops' Wars started in 1639 when Charles raised an army to overcome the Scots in an attempt to defy the National Covenant. The Scottish forces were called the Covenanters. The Bishops' Wars were part of the Scottish Revolution, which was part of the Wars of the Three Kingdoms. The Irish Confederate Wars and English Civil Wars were also part of the Wars of the Three Kingdoms—all of which started during the reign of Charles.

The Second Bishops' War took place in 1640, during which Charles experienced a major defeat and had to call the English Parliament to get further backing. The events that unfolded with Parliament led to the English Civil Wars from 1642 to 1651. Parliament and its allies were on the one side, while Charles and his allies were on the other. The Covenanters allied themselves with the English Parliament, and eventually Charles had to give himself up in submission.

He broke free from Parliamentary custody after the Covenanters handed him over to them. After fleeing across Britain, he eventually stationed himself on the Isle of Wight, where he negotiated with his army, the Scots, and the English Parliament to try and broker an understanding in 1647. In 1648 the last Scottish supporters of the king were killed, and in 1649 he was tried and executed for multiple offenses.

CHARLES II

Charles II was born in 1630 and had a comfortable upbringing during the first few years, including a good education. He was sent to France early in life to escape the violence that was taking place under Charles I's reign. When his father was executed in 1649, the Scottish crowned him their king. This was in violation of the sentiment of Cromwell's government in England. He agreed to the Presbyterian Covenant as a condition of his rule, which was a regulation that was anti-Anglican and anti-Catholic.

Oliver Cromwell was a powerful adversary. The Scots faced his New Model Army in 1650, which resulted in a great victory for the English. Charles II instigated an invasion into England in 1651, which also resulted in defeat for the Scots. The invasion left him with no choice but to flee to France where he had few connections, little access to money, and not many friends. His fortunes would change after Cromwell's death in 1658.

When Cromwell died, it left England with the problem of his strongest allies fighting to take over his position. The drastic solution was to place Charles II on the English throne in 1660, in what is now called the Restoration. He was given the crown on the condition that he meet multiple reforms laid out by Parliament. His rule was known for bringing a better compromise between the multiple religious factions of England—mainly Anglican, Catholic, and Nonconformist.

Little heed was paid to ruling the affairs of Scotland in comparison with those of England. He ruled until his death in 1685. He was succeeded by his brother as he had no legitimate children (although he had 14 illegitimate children, possibly many more).

JAMES VII

James VII was Charles II's brother. He was raised mainly in England, from which he fled in 1648 during the civil war. While abroad, he spent time at the Hague in the

Netherlands and then in France. He served in both the Spanish and French militaries. Unlike his brother, James VII was a Catholic. This caused some upheaval when he returned to England, resulting in him being sent to live in Brussels in the 1670s to pacify the public.

After Brussels, he was stationed in Edinburgh as the King's High Commissioner—a post he held from 1679 to 1682. When his brother died in 1685, he inherited both the English and Scottish crowns. He instituted a policy of religious tolerance for Catholics and Nonconformists and placed multiple Catholic individuals in official positions of his government. Unrest started breaking out because of the change from the Protestant state they had grown used to during the rules of his brother, father, grandfather, and Elizabeth I over the previous century.

A group of nobles invited William of Orange, who was married to his Protestant cousin (Mary), to invade England and remove James VII from power. William's invasion took place in 1688, which resulted in the Glorious Revolution. No blood was shed, and James VII fled to France. He tried to regain control of the crown in 1690 with forces that he gathered in Ireland. The forces were defeated at the Battle of the Boyne, after which James VII spent the rest of his life in exile in a palace near Paris.

WILLIAM III

William of Orange was born in 1650, two weeks after his father passed away. He inherited the position of head of the House of Orange. The house had power, connections, and money. When his mother died when he was 10 years old, the Dutch aristocracy and English royal family both tried to get custodianship of William. Ultimately, he remained in the Netherlands for the rest of his upbringing.

When he was a teenager and into his early twenties, the Netherlands were involved in a lot of warfare. The disaster year struck in 1672 when armies from multiple countries invaded the Netherlands, with the French getting right to its heart. Formalities were abandoned in the aftermath, and William was granted the position of stadtholder (ruler of the nation), adding to his existing role of heading the House of Orange. As stadtholder he formed peace arrangements with France and pacified the English by marrying Mary (the Protestant daughter of James VII).

William became a Protestant figurehead of Europe. He took the time to openly criticize the rule of his father-in-law in England as a Catholic king. Being such a figurehead, having Mary's hand in marriage, and being a grandson of Charles I made William a desirable replacement for James VII. A few nobles thus invited William to invade and depose his father-in-law. After the Glorious Revolution, Mary and William were crowned as joint monarchs of England, Scotland, Ireland, and the other realms of the kingdom in 1689. They ruled together until Mary's death in 1694, after which he ruled alone to his own death in 1702.

QUEEN ANNE

Queen Anne succeeded William of Orange as the crown's last Stuart (Stewart) monarch. She was born in 1665 as the second daughter of James VII (Mary of Orange's younger sister). She was a shy and pleasant individual, but of a sickly constitution. She married George, prince of Denmark, in 1683, with whom she had 17 pregnancies (one of which was successful). Their son, however, died at the age of 11.

As the last Protestant member of the line who was eligible for the throne, she was crowned when William of Orange died in 1702. Much of her rule was controlled by a council that governed on her behalf. During her reign, there were multiple major victories against France, and the union of Parliaments took place under the Acts of Union 1707. This period was one of uprising and violence in Scotland, as the majority of the public and nobles weren't in favor of the union. After she passed away in 1714, the crown moved to the Hanover line of monarchs.

THE UNION OF PARLIAMENTS

Unifying Parliaments of Scotland and England started being discussed in earnest in 1702 when Queen Anne took power. It was a hotly debated topic, with all sorts of nobles sending out pamphlets to advocate for their vested interests in the matter. Arguments for joining Parliaments were that it would bring Scotland access to England's colonies and it would reduce the amount of warfare they were exposed to. Those against the merge said that it would damage the country's sovereignty and that parliamentarians living in London would be both out of touch and less accountable to their constituents.

Formal negotiations were entered to determine the provisions of the union in 1706. As the provisions were announced, the existing tension in Scotland was exacerbated. Riots broke out, and the government started introducing regulations that outlawed the formation of crowds in some contexts. Parliamentarians and judges were jeered at by upset crowds. In retaliation people were told to keep their households in check, and punishments were meted out for offenders. In the end, negotiations ended, the Acts of Union were passed, and the Scottish Parliament was dissolved in 1707.

Some of the outcomes from the union were that the royal line of succession would have to run through Protestant rulers, the economies of the countries would be tied together, the legal system of courts of each country would remain under their own jurisdiction, and Scotland would regulate its own educational system. Parliaments were ultimately joined, and parliamentarians were sent to represent Scotland in London.

JACOBITE RISINGS

With the Glorious Revolution, James VII was removed from power in 1688. There were, however, multiple factions that still wanted him in power. The major faction was the Catholic church and its adherents. The Scottish Episcopalians were another as they were able to coexist in a less hostile environment under his rule. Some were also those loyal to the traditional line of Stewart kings. These supporters were called the Jacobites (Jacobite referring to an ancient rendition of the name James).

The Jacobites first rose up in 1689 with an army consisting largely of Highlander forces. They won at the Battle of Killiecrankie—their first major conflict. Further battles were waged during 1689 and 1690, resulting in defeat after defeat against the armies of William of Orange's new government. The Jacobites stayed largely subdued for the next 24 years. In 1714, George I of the Hanover line was placed on the throne.

The first major rising was called the Fifteen (due to it taking place in 1715). During the Fifteen, thousands of Jacobite Highlanders formed into an army and marched south. They faced their opponents in support of the Stewart who would have been king if the crown had remained in the family line—James Edward Stewart. The outcome of the conflict was uncertain, with the Jacobites losing the passion they had for the cause. The passion couldn't be rekindled, even when James Edward Stewart landed in Scotland later that year. It would be 30 years before the next Jacobite rising took place.

In 1745, the charismatic son of James Edward Stewart—fondly called Bonnie Prince Charlie—landed at the Outer Hebrides to start building support for claiming the throne. He gathered a Highlander army that he led to victory against the government's army in Edinburgh. They continued south but couldn't manage to gather enough support in England, so they returned to Scotland. At the Battle of Culloden in 1746, the army faced the troops of the duke of Cumberland along with government soldiers. A bloodbath ensued with Bonnie Prince Charlie's fighters being executed after the battle for treason.

He fled to mainland Europe, and the Jacobite cause didn't gather any future momentum. James Edward Stewart died in 1766, while the Bonnie Prince died in 1788. With their deaths, the cause of the Jacobites went cold.

This chapter looked at the end of an age of passion for the Scottish monarchy and fighting for independence. The next chapter shows how the Scottish refocused during the coming periods of the Industrial Revolution and the Modern Era. A lot was accomplished, and a lot of change took place.

CHAPTER 5
THE MODERN ERA

In this chapter three of the most important parts of Scotland's modern history will be examined. The first is the Industrial Revolution and how it benefited the nation. The Highland Clearances will be the second topic we look into, with a subsection covering how Scotland's diaspora has spread across the globe. The final part will examine how Scottish nationalism has become a more relevant topic over the last century and the key events that have taken place along this line.

THE INDUSTRIAL REVOLUTION IN SCOTLAND

Prior to the Industrial Revolution, Scotland had a rural and agricultural economy. This was set to change when the Chemical Revolution took place in the 1750s. At the time, a professor of chemistry for the universities of Edinburgh and Glasgow (Joseph Black) had made a discovery. He had isolated carbon dioxide, which he detailed in a thesis he published in 1756. This thesis had the deeper significance of showing that you could isolate elements from a substance to make them purer. The discovery led to a small boom of isolating other elements, specifically oxygen, hydrogen, chlorine, and nitrogen.

Making use of these discoveries, Joseph worked with another professor (William Cullen) to form a substance from chlorine that would speed up the process of linen bleaching. The efficiency of the bleaching process made Scotland a more competitive nation in the linen industry. Soon other developments were incorporated into the process of linen making, advancements that had mainly come from England. They included the water frame, the spinning jenny, and the mule. A resultant rapid increase in the linen production industry made Scotland a global industry leader.

Soon thereafter, the factory system was developed in Scotland. It made use of cheap labor, combined with machine production, to produce large amounts of linen more efficiently. Cotton largely replaced linen as it could be made into finer cloth. Imports of cotton obtained from India and other English colonies were processed in the Scottish factories (mainly by women and child labor at low rates of pay). Final products were then exported to European and American markets, establishing an international trade route in the process.

The next major industry in which Scotland became a leader was tobacco supply. Agents took tools and other developments to the American and West Indies plantations and obtained tobacco in return. The developments and tools led to more efficient production of tobacco and better stockpiles.

Soon a system developed wherein the Scottish agents would pick up slaves in Africa; then take the slaves, tools, and other things to the plantations in the West; and return with tobacco from the stockpiles on the plantations. When the stockpiles reached Scotland, tobacco would be sold to markets in Europe and beyond. In short order, they dominated the tobacco trade due to faster turnaround times than those of other tobacco traders in other nations. The sugar industry soon followed in the same fashion.

Developments took place in the banking industry because of this increase in trade. The banks in Scotland had large amounts of money from the trade and industry taking place. As such, they innovated things such as the bank overdraft. During the same era, a Scotsman named Adam Smith wrote The Wealth of Nations—the book that formed the foundation of capitalism. With the innovations taking place in the Scottish economy and banking sector, he developed the principles that guide free trade up to this day.

A last major Industrial Revolution development from Scotland was attributable to James Watt. He advanced the technology of steam engines, allowing them to work more efficiently. Less water would be required to power engines and factories as a result, while their output became more powerful. Soon the first passenger steamship was made (1812), after which Scotland would later become the world's most productive manufacturer of ships. The first steam train was also innovated, leading to railways, which formed the backbone of cheap transport for the world's developing industries.

THE HIGHLAND CLEARANCES AND THE SCOTTISH DIASPORA

From the 1750s, large farming estates of the Highlands started undergoing processes to make them more efficient. They were drained and enclosed, crop rotation was implemented on a large scale, and cattle were swapped with sheep. Farm outputs and profits increased, but this would all come at the expense of the comfort and livelihoods of families.

In the 1780s, the populations of farms were relocated to other parts of the estate, usually to small farms called crofts on the seaside. The people were evicted (sometimes by burning down their past homes on the estate) with the expectation that they would make their livelihoods on fishing and kelping. They were to provide rent for the crofts they were allotted.

The developments of the Industrial Revolution contributed to the situation. The mindset that production was everything had taken hold, and land efficiency became more important than ever. Those that got in the way were a necessary sacrifice in return for profit.

Successful urbanization had taken place in lower parts of the country, so many Highland estate owners thought they could produce the same results. The changes in the economic situation of the relocated Highlanders were serious because the crofts could not provide the output they needed to support their food requirements. To make matters worse, the Great Highland Famine took place in the mid-nineteenth century, with blight affecting the potato harvests.

The result was the croft communities couldn't support themselves and needed to rely on charity for survival and they couldn't afford the rent due to estate owners for use of the crofts. The kinder landowners paid for the relocation of their tenants to better lands to the southern areas of Scotland, while more cruel landowners simply evicted them. The lower population, along with other economic factors, meant that croft settlements could sustain themselves for the third quarter of the nineteenth century and could pay their rent. Soon, however, depression hit and weather conditions had a negative impact on their output. The Crofters' War of the 1880s resulted.

The government and general public sympathized with and even supported the crofters, with a solution being demanded. The solution came in the form of a government investigation, followed by passing of the Crofters Holdings (Scotland) Act. It provided holistic interventions that offered some relief. Rental debt from crofters was adjudicated and adjusted, payment plans were worked out, security was provided against eviction, the Crofters Commission was established to judge disputes between landlords and crofters, and crofters were allowed to keep the benefits of extensions to their crofts.

By the end of the nineteenth century, further government provisions were made to alleviate conditions. The government purchased some of the land from their landlords with the intention of benefiting the crofters. Both agricultural and transportation infrastructure were improved. This solution was partly successful, but problems still remained. A definite sense of class division developed, along with the sense that lords of Highland land didn't care about their people. The Highlands are still dotted with the shells of buildings that were evicted in the clearances.

THE SPREAD OF THE SCOTTISH DIASPORA

There had been a spread of Scottish people to other countries throughout the nation's history. A notable example is the settling of Scottish mercenaries in France after the Auld Alliance.

The formation of the Ulster Plantation and other plantations in Ireland during the sixteenth and seventeenth centuries led to more displacement of the Scottish. The English government wanted to make sure that the Irish were subdued by spreading English and Scottish people and ideas in their midst. They disestablished many Irish communities, particularly those that fell on the lands of nobles who had supported anti-English movements. Not only was it useful for the government to bring a more direct non-Irish presence in their homeland but it was used as an opportunity to get rid of people who were causing trouble in Scotland. Many of the more independent-minded people of the Highlands were forcibly removed to the plantations where they were to establish their own communities among the Irish and English.

The number increased during the time of the Industrial Revolution. Many of the people involved in trade or being agents of other people or organizations (such as in the tobacco trade) found that they could establish comfortable lives abroad for themselves and their families. Permanent settlement wasn't too uncommon an occurrence. Add to this the exodus of people from northern and western Scotland during the Highland Clearances, and many people jumped on opportunities to settle where they would have better chances of comfortable living. The fact remains, however, that there were people from other regions of Scotland who also wanted to seek their own place in the wide world.

Immigration from Scotland has remained steady throughout the Late Modern Era. People leave the country mainly to move to other parts of the United Kingdom, Canada, Australia, or New Zealand. People's reasons vary, but the fact remains that even at present more than 20% of those born in Scotland have immigrated (The Scotsman, 2016).

THE RISE OF SCOTTISH NATIONALISM AND THE CURRENT POLITICAL SITUATION IN SCOTLAND

Nationalism existed throughout the history of Scotland. Support of the identity of the nation was important to individuals throughout the ages. This started right from the creation of Alba, or perhaps earlier. National pride increased through the centuries, and symbols of the Scottish nation served to unify its people.

The crown (and royal family) was one such symbol, the Stone of Destiny another, as well as the Scottish flag. There were many others. Their unique identity set them apart from neighbors like the Irish, English, or groups that could have been their predecessors (e.g., the Picts). It united all people of the nation, from the townies in southern Scotland to the Highlanders of the north.

The Scottish nation's sense of self remained in spite of the trouble it had faced with English overlordship since before the Wars of Scottish Independence. When the crown was joined with that of England under James VI, the Scottish identity remained. The unification of Parliaments under Queen Anne didn't sway the distinctiveness of the Scottish nation. Neither did intermarrying the royal family with other regal families—such as Mary's (Queen of Scots) marriage to Francis II of France.

Failure to establish a colony in Panama (in the seventeenth century), known as the Darien scheme, could have destroyed the country's morale. However, it served to bring its citizens closer because they knew they weren't helped in their hour of need and they knew their English-centered monarch wasn't going to advance their well-being as much as they could themselves. The Darien scheme involved investments from almost every individual in Scotland who was able to donate a bit of money. When the settlement failed because of financial trouble (from English and foreign investors pulling out), illness, and a rough environment, the Scottish rallied and focused on forming a strong nation locally.

The Jacobite risings of the seventeenth and eighteenth centuries were an endeavor largely the result of Scottish nationalism. The forces of the risings were made up largely of Highlanders who were loyal to the Stuart (Stewart) family as it originally held power in Scotland. When these failed and the union was sealed, the Kirk (Church of Scotland) became the nation's uniting symbol by enforcing its separateness from the Anglican church and becoming a center of guidance for both nobles and common people. The Industrial Revolution of the eighteenth century also became a uniting force.

Scotland started advancing faster than almost any other nation in the world in science and other spheres. They were miles ahead of England in terms of new discoveries and the presence of tertiary education institutions. The nation was becoming highly urbanized and had become a world leader in the linen, sugar, and tobacco trades. Infrastructure was being implemented at a rate never seen before, with Scottish cities becoming global urban front-runners.

Home rule became a more enticing prospect during the nineteenth century. Scotland had been an active member of the United Kingdom during the advances of the Industrial Revolution and Late Modern Period, with benefits from England and its Commonwealth being clear. Despite the benefits, a locally based government would possibly be more accountable and provide better service to its people, and a local parliament would bring more relevant legislation. Further, warfare with Ireland as it was fighting for independence showed that there weren't as many benefits to staying in the United Kingdom as they had thought. The independence that Ireland won at the start of the twentieth century showed independence to have its own benefits, even for a nation that had been a long-term member of the United Kingdom.

The Scottish Nationalist Party was formed in 1934. It gained gradual support over the next two decades, with infighting being the major problem to its initial growth. The expansion of the party slowed, and it didn't hold much influence until the 1970s when oil was discovered off the Scottish coast—oil that could provide a veritable economic goldmine. The referendum of 1979 for devolution of Parliament garnered a lot of support, but not enough for anything to materialize. A referendum was executed again in 1997, this time with a successful vote.

Parliament was devolved, with its first sitting in 1999 in Edinburgh. Progress started snowballing, with the Scottish Nationalist Party gaining the majority government of Scotland in 2011, resulting in another referendum in 2014 for total independence. The referendum had 45% support from voters, showing that nearly half of the country wanted full autonomy. Despite not gaining full independence, further powers were given to the Scottish Parliament to regulate its own affairs. While it's not clear whether full autonomy will occur or not, the topic is certainly an engaging one to observe.

CONCLUSION

This book delved into the deepest parts of Scottish history. The prehistoric people who settled in the area of the modern nation were examined in depth. You were shown how they lived their lives and what types of tools they used to survive. The development of those people and further migrations into the area during the New Stone Age, Bronze Age, and Iron Age were surveyed. Once the prehistoric peoples had been analyzed, we looked at the prehistoric Celtic tribes that settled where Scotland is today.

The Celtic tribes were scanned one by one. Not much is known about the tribes as they used oral traditions rather than written records. That said, archeological evidence and writings from Roman records gave some idea about their identities. The attempts of the Romans to overcome the northernmost tribes of Britain showed that they might have had some military success, but they were never able to keep the tribes completely under their control. The tribal groups that managed to keep their identities strong developed into the Scotti, Picts, and Britons.

The Scotti and their kingdom of Dalriada were the predecessors of the Scottish nation today. While the Picts provided strong opponents, they seemed to have been absorbed into the Scotti kingdom, resulting in the formation of Alba. The Brittonic tribes of the Scottish regions—mainly

Strathclyde—were overcome and likewise absorbed into the cultural union of the Scotti and Picts. The kingdom that emerged was first called Alba, and then the name gradually changed to Scotland.

The royal line of Alba and Scotland was documented, showing the major impacts of each monarch. The historical developments, uprisings, and periods that took place during their reigns were linked to each other. The main characters of those events, such as the Scottish Reformation, were briefly discussed to give a more complete understanding of the times. This culminated in a review of the end of the monarchy's presence in Scotland with the union of the crowns and the union of Parliaments.

The birth of Scotland as a nation without a figurehead in the country meant the Kirk became its central institution. The warfare that resulted to protect the Kirk and attempts to bring the Stewart line of monarchs back into power showed how the identity of the nation had remained prominent throughout the centuries. This led to looking at the developments of the Modern Era that impacted Scotland as a state—the Industrial Revolution, the Highland Clearances, and strengthened Scottish nationalism.

Scotland was a key player in the Industrial Revolution. There were so many discoveries made, with some of the ones included in the book being isolation of chemical elements, enhancement of production with the factory process, and improved linen and cotton production methodologies. The wealth this brought into the nation led to a focus on efficiency and building the wealth of the nation. One of the unfortunate effects of this was the Highland Clearances, in which the rights of humans were relegated to a junior level next to efficient use of land and financial profits.

As a result of the Highland Clearances and other circumstances, both nationally and internationally, immigration became a norm. This was partly due to the opportunities that were available as a result of being a member of the United Kingdom and reaping the benefits of her colonies. Despite this, the identity of Scotland as a sovereign state gradually regained support. Over the last century, nationalism has become a more relevant issue, resulting in the devolution of the Scottish Parliament in 1999 and more than one referendum regarding independent governance.

This book showed the key historical events and figures of Scotland. The information wasn't made unnecessarily complex, yet it also wasn't presented in an oversimplified manner. The aim was to present the material in a neutral fashion, but focusing mainly on Scottish history itself, rather than the history of the United Kingdom, England, or other players. Where information about other nations was included, it was to provide context of impacts directly within Scotland. With a deeper understanding of its history, it was shown that the Scottish people have a far more complex and sophisticated heritage than they are often made out to have.

With this book, it is our hope that you both enjoyed learning about the past of this nation and gained a perspective as to where the nation is advancing toward. There are many nuances to the Scottish race, whom you now have a well-rounded perspective about.

APPENDIX 1
LIST OF SCOTTISH KINGS AND QUEENS

Scota (with the Egyptian name Neferubity, who was a daughter of the fictional pharaoh Chencres, who is possibly the historical pharaoh Thutmose I) and Gaythelos (a Greek prince) were said to be the original founders of what would become the Scottish nation. They sailed away from Egypt and landed in the Iberian Peninsula. The couple had, among other children, a son named Hyber. He was said to be the one whom the ancient name of Ireland—Hibernia—comes from. They established a city named Brigancia (possibly the modern city of A Coruña).

It is said that there were multiple generations that lived in Brigancia. A lot of warfare took place with the local people of Iberia, with some of Scota's descendants and their followers deciding to leave. Some settled in Ireland, and others traveled further to settle in Scotland. Scota and Gaythelos were thus thought to be the progenitors of the Scottish nation, including the monarchs.

MYTHICAL MONARCHS PRIOR TO THE FOUNDING OF ALBA

BEFORE COMMON ERA

- Fergus I (330–305)
- Feritharis (305–290)
- Mainus (290–261)
- Dornadilla (261–233)
- Nothatus (233–213)
- Reutherus (213–187)
- Reutha (187-170)
- Thereus (170–161)
- Josina (161–137)
- Finnanus (137–107)
- Durstus (107–98)
- Evenus I (98–79)
- Gillus (79–77)
- Evenus II (77–60)
- Ederus (60–12)
- Evenus III (12–4)
- Metallanus (4 B.C.E.-35)

COMMON ERA

- Caratacus (35–55)
- Corbred I (55–72)
- Dardanus (72–76)
- Corbred II (76–110)
- Luctacus (110–113)
- Mogaldus (113–149)
- Conarus (149–163)
- Ethodius I (163–195)
- Satrael (195–199)
- Donald I (199–216)

- Ethodius II (216–231)
- Athirco (231–242)
- Nathalocus (242–253)
- Indochus (253–264)
- Donald II (264–265)
- Donald III (265–277)
- Crathilinthus (277–301)
- Fincormachus (301–348)
- Romachus (348–351)
- Angusianus (351–353)
- Fethelmacus (353–357)
- Eugenius I (357–404)
- Fergus II (404–420)
- Eugenius II (420–452)
- Dongardus (452–457)
- Constantine I (457–479)
- Congallus I (479–501)
- Goranus (501–535)
- Eugenius III (535–558)
- Congallus II (558–568)
- Kinnatellus (568–569)
- Aidanus (569–604)
- Kenneth I (604–605)
- Eugenius IV (605–622)
- Ferchard I (622–635)
- Donald IV (635–648)
- Ferchard II (648–668)
- Maldvinus (668–684)
- Eugenius V (684–688)
- Eugenius VI (688–698)
- Amberkelethus (698–699)
- Eugenius VII (699-716)
- Mordacus (716–731)
- Etfinus (731–761)
- Eugenius VIII (761–764)
- Fergus III (764–767)

- Solvathius (767–787)
- Achaius (787–819)
- Congallus III (819–824)
- Dongallus (824–830)
- Alpinus (830–833)

MONARCHS FROM THE FOUNDING OF ALBA TO THE UNIFICATION OF THE CROWNS

- Kenneth I MacAlpin (843–858)
- Donald I (858–862)
- Constantine I (862–877)
- Aed (877–878)
- Eochaid and Giric (878-889)
- Donald II (889–900)
- Constantine II (900–943)
- Malcolm I (943–954)
- Indulf (954–962)
- Dub (962–967)
- Culen (967–971)
- Kenneth II (971–995)
- Constantine III (995–997)
- Kenneth III (997–1005)
- Malcolm II (1005–1034)
- Duncan I (1034–1040)
- Macbeth (1040–1057)
- Lulach (1057–1058)
- Malcolm III Canmore (1058–1093)
- Donald Bane (1093–1094)
- Duncan II (1093–1094)
- Donald Bane (1094–1097)
- Edgar (1097–1107)
- Alexander I (1107–1124)
- David I (1124–1153)
- Malcolm IV (1153–1165)

- William I the Lion (1165–1214)
- Alexander II (1214–1249)
- Alexander III (1249–1286)
- Margaret, Maid of Norway (1286–1290)
- John Balliol (1292–1296)
- Robert I the Bruce (1306–1329)
- David II (1329–1371)
- Robert II (1371–1390)
- Robert III (1390–1406)
- James I (1406–1437)
- James II (1437–1460)
- James III (1460–1488)
- James IV (1488–1513)
- James V (1513–1542)
- Mary, Queen of Scots (1542–1567)
- James VI (1567–1625)
- (The union of the crowns occurred under James VI, resulting in a joint monarchy between England and Scotland.)

APPENDIX 2
LIST OF MAJOR BATTLES AND WARS

- Mons Graupius (84)
- Battle of Degsastan (603)
- Battle of Nechtansmere (685)
- Battle of Athelstaneford (832)
- McAlpin's Treason (841) (legend—likely untrue)
- Battle of Brunanburh (937)
- Battle of Luncarty (980)
- Battle of Mortlach (1010)
- Battle of Carham (1018)
- Battle of Lumphanan (1057)
- Battle of Essie (1058)
- Battle of Alnwick (1093)
- Battle of Mondynes (1094)
- Battle of the Standard (1138)
- Battle of Largs (1263)
- Battle of Dunbar (1296) (First War of Scottish Independence)
- Capture of Kinclaven Castle (1297) (First War of Scottish Independence)
- Battle of Stirling Bridge (1297) (First War of Scottish Independence)
- Battle of Falkirk (1298) (First War of Scottish Independence)
- Siege of Caerlaverock Castle (1300) (First War of Scottish Independence)
- Battle of Roslin Glen (1303) (First War of Scottish Independence)
- Siege of Stirling Castle (1304) (First War of Scottish Independence)

- Battle of Methven (1306) (First War of Scottish Independence)
- Battle of Dalry (1306)
- Battle of Loudoun Hill (1307) (First War of Scottish Independence)
- Battle of Glentrool (1307) (First War of Scottish Independence)
- Battle of Barra (1308) (First War of Scottish Independence)
- Battle of the Pass of Brander (1308) (First War of Scottish Independence)
- Battle of Bannockburn (1314) (First War of Scottish Independence)
- Battle of Dundalk (1318) (First War of Scottish Independence)
- Battle of Old Byland (1322) (First War of Scottish Independence)
- The Weardale Campaign (1327) (First War of Scottish Independence)
- Battle of Teba (1330)
- Battle of Dupplin Moor (1332) (Second War of Scottish Independence)
- Battle of Annan (1332) (Wars of the Three Kingdoms)
- Battle of Kinghorn (1332)
- Battle of Halidon Hill (1333) (Second War of Scottish Independence)
- Battle of Culblean (1335) (Second War of Scottish Independence)
- Battle of Neville's Cross (1346) (Second War of Scottish Independence)
- Battle of Nesbit Moor (1355)
- Battle of Benrig (1380) (Second War of Scottish Independence)
- Battle of Otterburn (1388) (Anglo-Scottish Wars)
- Battle of the Clans (1396)
- Battle of Nesbit Moor (1402)
- Battle of Homildon Hill (1402) (Hundred-Year War)
- Battle of Harlaw (1411)
- Battle of Yeavering (1415)
- Battle of Lochaber (1429)
- First Battle of Inverlochy (1431)
- Battle of Piperdean (1436)
- Battle of Sark (1448) (Hundred-Year War)
- Battle of Brechin Muir (1452)
- Battle of Clachnaharry (1454)

- Battle of Arkinholm (1455)
- Siege of Roxburgh (1460)
- Battle of Tannach Moor (1464)
- Battle of Bloody Bay (1480)
- Battle of Lochmaben Fair (1484)
- Battle of Sauchieburn (1488)
- Battle of Gartalunane (1489)
- Battle of Flodden (1513)
- Battle of Hornshole (1514)
- Battle of Melrose (1526)
- Battle of Linlithgow Bridge (1526)
- Battle of Solway Moss (1542)
- Battle of the Shirts (1544)
- Battle of Ancrum Moor (1545) (War of the Rough Wooing)
- Battle of Pinkie Cleugh (1547)
- Siege of Haddington (1548) (War of the Rough Wooing)
- Battle of Corrichie (1562)
- Battle of Carberry Hill (1567)
- Battle of Langside (1568) (Marian Civil War)
- Lang Siege (1571) (Marian Civil War)
- Battle of Tillieangus (1571) (Marian Civil War)
- Redeswire Raid (1575)
- Eigg Massacre (1577)
- Blar Na Leine (1578)
- Blar Milleadh Garaidh (1578)
- Battle of Glenlivet (1594)
- Battle of Glenfruin (1603)
- Loch Earn Raid (1620)
- Battle of Megray Hill (1639) (First Bishops' War)
- Battle of Newburn Ford (1640) (Second Bishops' War)
- Battle of Tippermuir (1644) (Wars of the Three Kingdoms)
- Battle of Aberdeen (1644) (Wars of the Three Kingdoms)
- Battle of Inverlochy (1645) (Wars of the Covenant)
- Battle of Auldearn (1645) (Scottish Civil War)
- Battle of Alford (1645) (Scottish Civil War)
- Battle of Kilsyth (1645) (Scottish Civil War)

- Battle of Philiphaugh (1645) (Scottish Civil War)
- Battle of Mauchline Moor (1648) (Scottish Civil War)
- Battle of Preston (1648) (English Civil Wars)
- Battle of Carbisdale (1650) (Wars of the Three Kingdoms)
- Battle of Dunbar (1650) (English Civil Wars)
- Battle of Worcester (1651) (English Civil Wars)
- Battle of Pitreavie (1651)
- Battle of Dundee (1651) (English Civil Wars)
- Battle of Inverkeithing (1651) (Wars of the Three Kingdoms)
- Battle of Dalnaspidal (1654) (Wars of the Three Kingdoms)
- Battle of Strone Nevis (1654)
- Battle of Rullion Green (1666) (Wars of the Three Kingdoms)
- Battle of Drumclog (1679) (Scottish Covenanter Wars)
- Battle of Bothwell Bridge (1679) (Scottish Covenanter Wars)
- Battle of Airds Moss (1680)
- The Glorious Revolution (1688) (nobody died, giving it the alternate name of the Bloodless Revolution)
- Battle of Mulroy (1688)
- Battle of Killiecrankie (1689) (Jacobite risings)
- Battle of Dunkeld (1689) (Jacobite risings)
- Battle of Boyne (1690) (Jacobite risings)
- Battle of Cromdale (1690) (Jacobite risings)
- Glencoe Massacre (1692)
- Battle of Sheriffmuir (1715) (Jacobite risings)
- Battle of Preston (1715) (Jacobite risings)
- Battle of Glenshiel (1719) (Jacobite risings)
- Glasgow Malt-Tax Riots (1725)
- Porteous Riots (1736)
- Battle of Prestonpans (1745) (Jacobite risings)
- Battle of Inverurie (1745) (Jacobite risings)
- Battle of Falkirk Muir (1746) (Jacobite risings)
- Battle of Culloden (1746) (Jacobite risings)
- Battle of the Braes (1882)

REFERENCES

Abernethy, S. (2018, July 13). *Joan of the Tower, Queen of Scots.* The
    Freelance History Writer.
    https://thefreelancehistorywriter.com/2018/07/13/joan-of-the-
    tower-queen-of-scots/
About: Battle of Aberdeen (1644). (n.d.). DBpedia.
    https://dbpedia.org/page/Battle_of_Aberdeen_(1644)
About: Battle of Alford. (n.d.). DBpedia.
    https://dbpedia.org/page/Battle_of_Alford
About: Battle of Annan Moor. (n.d.). DBpedia.
    https://dbpedia.org/page/Battle_of_Annan_Moor
About: Battle of Dalnaspidal. (n.d.). DBpedia.
    https://dbpedia.org/page/Battle_of_Dalnaspidal
About: Battle of Dalrigh. (n.d.). DBpedia.
    https://dbpedia.org/page/Battle_of_Dalrigh
About: Battle of Kinghorn. (n.d.). DBpedia.
    https://dbpedia.org/page/Battle_of_Kinghorn
About: Dub, King of Scotland. (n.d.). DBpedia.
    https://dbpedia.org/page/Dub,_King_of_Scotland
A brief history of the Jacobite risings. (n.d.). Sky HISTORY.
    https://www.history.co.uk/articles/a-brief-history-of-the-
    jacobite-risings
Act of Union 1707. (n.d.). UK Parliament.
    https://www.parliament.uk/about/living-
    heritage/evolutionofparliament/legislativescrutiny/act-of-union-
    1707/#:~:text=The%20Acts%20of%20Union%2C%20passed
Act of Union 1707: Contemporary context. (2016, August). UK Parliament.
    https://www.parliament.uk/about/living-

heritage/evolutionofparliament/legislativescrutiny/act-of-union-1707/contemporary-context/

Aed (877–878). (n.d.). ScotClans. https://www.scotclans.com/pages/aed-877-878

Aidan. (2020, June 24). *The lost kingdom of the Britons in Scotland*. Celtic Cross. https://www.celticcrossonline.com/the-lost-kingdom-of-the-britons-in-scotland/

Ashley, M. (2023). *Charles I*. Britannica. https://www.britannica.com/biography/Charles-I-king-of-Great-Britain-and-Ireland

Augustyn, A. (2023). *William II*. Britannica. https://www.britannica.com/biography/William-II-king-of-England

Battle of Auldearn. (n.d.). Wikiwand. https://www.wikiwand.com/en/Battle_of_Auldearn

Battle of Carbisdale. (n.d.). Military Wiki. https://military-history.fandom.com/wiki/Battle_of_Carbisdale

Battle of Homildon Hill. (n.d.). British Battles. https://www.britishbattles.com/one-hundred-years-war/battle-of-homildon-hill/

Battle of Inverkeithing. (n.d.). Military Wiki. https://military-history.fandom.com/wiki/Battle_of_Inverkeithing

Battle of Kilsyth. (n.d.). Historic Environment Scotland. http://portal.historicenvironment.scot/designation/BTL13

Battle of Luncarty. (n.d.). Electric Scotland. https://electricscotland.com/history/wars/04BattleOfLuncarty980.pdf

Battle of Philiphaugh. (n.d.). Battlefields Hub. https://www.battlefieldstrust.com/resource-centre/civil-war/battleview.asp?BattleFieldId=74

Battle of Sark. (n.d.). Historic Environment Scotland. http://portal.historicenvironment.scot/designation/BTL40

Battle site of Athelstaneford (832). (n.d.). Scotland's Finest. https://www.scotlandsfinest.nl/what-s-to-see/scotland-s-finest-battle-sites/battle-site-of-athelstaneford

Baury, R., Legay, M. (2009). *L'invention de la décentralisation: Noblesse et pouvoirs intermédiaires en France et en Europe xviie-xixe siècle*. Presses universitaires du Septentrion.

Bloks, M. (2017, November 23). *Gruoch – The real Lady Macbeth*. History of Royal Women. https://www.historyofroyalwomen.com/gruoch/gruoch-real-lady-macbeth/

Brain, J. (n.d.). *William of Orange*. Historic UK. https://www.historic-uk.com/HistoryUK/HistoryofEngland/William-Of-Orange/

Bronze Age. (n.d.). ScotClans. https://www.scotclans.com/pages/bronze-age

Buchanan, G. (1799). *The history of Scotland from the earliest accounts of that nation, to the reign of king James VI*. https://ia800205.us.archive.org/26/items/historyofscotlan02buch/historyofscotlan02buch.pdf

Buchanan, G. (1799). *The history of Scotland: from the earliest accounts of that nation, to the reign of King James VI*. Internet Archive. https://archive.org/details/historyofscotlan01buch/page/10/mode/2up

Buchanan, G. (n.d.). *The history of Scotland written in Latin by George Buchanan ; faithfully rendered into English*. Early English Books Online. https://quod.lib.umich.edu/e/eebo/A29962.0001.001/1:7?rgn=div1

Butler, J. (n.d.). *The Great Heathen Army*. Historic UK. https://www.historic-uk.com/HistoryUK/HistoryofEngland/Great-Heathen-Army/

Campbell, M. (n.d.). *History and heritage of Cumbria and the Lake District*. Kingfisher Visitor Guides. https://kingfishervisitorguides.com/features/history-and-heritage-of-cumbria-and-the-lake-district/

Cannon, J. A. (n.d.). *Gododdin, kingdom of the*. Encyclopedia.com. https://www.encyclopedia.com/history/encyclopedias-almanacs-transcripts-and-maps/gododdin-kingdom

Cartwright, M. (2022, January 25). *Battle of Preston in 1648*. World History Encyclopedia. https://www.worldhistory.org/article/1934/battle-of-preston-in-1648/

Castelow, E. (n.d.-a). *The Battle of Ancrum Moor*. Historic UK. https://www.historic-uk.com/HistoryMagazine/DestinationsUK/The-Battle-of-Ancrum-Moor/

Castelow, E. (n.d.-b). *The Battle of Bothwell Bridge*. Historic UK. https://www.historic-uk.com/HistoryMagazine/DestinationsUK/The-Battle-of-Bothwell-Bridge/

Castelow, E. (n.d.-c). *The Battle of Dupplin Moor*. Historic UK. https://www.historic-uk.com/HistoryMagazine/DestinationsUK/The-Battle-of-Dupplin-Moor/

Castelow, E. (n.d.-d). *The Battle of Otterburn*. Historic UK. https://www.historic-uk.com/HistoryMagazine/DestinationsUK/The-Battle-of-Otterburn/

Castelow, E. (n.d.-e). *The Battle of Worcester*. Historic UK. https://www.historic-uk.com/HistoryMagazine/DestinationsUK/The-Battle-of-Worcester/

Cheney, B., Thompson, P. M., Ingram, S. N., Hammond, P. S., Stevick, P. T., Durban, J. W., Culloch, R. M., Elwen, S. H., Mandleberg, L., Janik, V. M., Quick, N. J., ISLAS-Villanueva, V., Robinson, K. P., Costa, M., Eisfeld, S. M., Walters, A., Phillips, C., Weir, C. R., Evans, P. G. H., & Anderwald, P. (2012). Integrating multiple data sources to assess the distribution and abundance of bottlenose dolphins Tursiops truncatus in Scottish waters. *Mammal Review*, 43(1), 71–88. https://doi.org/10.1111/j.1365-2907.2011.00208.x

Clan Bruce. (n.d.). VisitScotland. https://www.visitscotland.com/info/see-do/clan-bruce-p1475091#:~:text=Clan%20Bruce%20was%20one%20of

Consequences of union. (n.d.). NLS Digital Gallery. https://digital.nls.uk/unionofcrowns/consequences.html

Cracknie souterrain. (n.d.). Forestry and Land Scotland. https://forestryandland.gov.scot/what-we-do/biodiversity-and-conservation/historic-environment-conservation/investigation/cracknie-souterrain#:~:text=The%20word%20comes%20from%20the

Cromdale battlefield. (n.d.). The Jacobite Trail. https://www.jacobitetrail.co.uk/cromdale-battlefield

Dalriada. (n.d.). The Scottish History Society. https://scottishhistorysociety.com/dalriada/

Damnoni Celtic tribe. (n.d.). Roman Britain. https://www.roman-britain.co.uk/tribes/damnoni/

Damnonii. (n.d.). Encyclopedia.com. https://www.encyclopedia.com/history/encyclopedias-almanacs-transcripts-and-maps/damnonii

Davies, J. R. (2019, August 18). *The absolution of Robert I, 1310.* The Community of the Realm of Scotland, 1249–1424. https://cotr.ac.uk/blog/absolution-robert-i-1310/

Devorgilla, Lady of Galloway. (n.d.). Undiscovered Scotland. https://www.undiscoveredscotland.co.uk/usbiography/d/devorgilla.html

Documenting the Union of Parliaments. (n.d.). National Library of Scotland. https://www.nls.uk/collections/rare-books/collections/union-of-parliaments/

Donald I (860-863). (n.d.). ScotClans. https://www.scotclans.com/pages/donald-i-860-863

Dumbarton Castle. (n.d.). Historic Environment Scotland. https://www.historicenvironment.scot/visit-a-place/places/dumbarton-castle/history/#:~:text=Its%20recorded%20history%20goes%20back

Duncan, Brian. (2012). *Scottish nationalism: The symbols of Scottish distinctiveness and the 700 Year continuum of the Scots' desire for self determination.* JMU Scholarly Commons. https://commons.lib.jmu.edu/master201019/192

English heritage battlefield report: Newburn Ford 1640. (1995). Historic England. https://historicengland.org.uk/content/docs/listing/battlefields/newburn-ford/

Epidii Celtic tribe. (n.d.). Roman Britain. https://www.roman-britain.co.uk/tribes/the-epidii-or-epidi/

Erik II. (n.d.). Britannica. https://www.britannica.com/biography/Erik-II

Family tree Cromer/Russell/Buck/Pratt» Kenneth I McAlpin of Scotland (810--858). (n.d.). Genealogy Online. https://www.genealogieonline.nl/en/family-tree-cromer-russell-buck-pratt/P23470.php

Fergus I, king of Scotland (330–305 B.C.). (n.d.). Royal Collection Trust. https://www.rct.uk/collection/403322/fergus-i-king-of-scotland-330-305-b-c

FlikeNoir. (2018, May 22). *What happened to the Scottish monarchy?* Random Scottish History. https://randomscottishhistory.com/2018/05/22/what-happened-to-the-scottish-monarchy/

Fraser, A. (2023). *Mary.* Britannica. https://www.britannica.com/biography/Mary-queen-of-Scotland

Gaels and Scots. (n.d.). The Book of Deer Project. http://bookofdeer.co.uk/historical-background/gaels-and-scots/

Garlinghouse, T. (2022, August 17). *Who were the Picts, the early inhabitants of Scotland?* Live Science. https://www.livescience.com/who-were-picts-scotland

Hayes, A. (2022, June 8). Adam Smith and "the wealth of nations." Investopedia. https://www.investopedia.com/updates/adam-smith-wealth-of-nations/

Hepburn, D. (2023, March 17). *Biggest towns in Scotland: Here are the 21 largest Scottish towns by population – from Paisley to Newton Mearns.* The Scotsman. https://www.scotsman.com/lifestyle/family-and-parenting/biggest-towns-in-scotland-here-are-the-21-largest-scottish-towns-by-population-from-paisley-to-newton-mearns-4069525

History. (n.d.). Scotland. https://www.scotland.org/about-scotland/history-timeline

History of the Stewarts | Battles and historic events. (n.d.). The Stewart Society. https://www.stewartsociety.org/history-of-the-stewarts.cfm?section=battles-and-historical-events&subcatid=1&histid=443

Hosch, W. L. (2023). *Bishops' Wars.* Britannica. https://www.britannica.com/event/Bishops-Wars

Iron Age – Celts, Picts and Romans. (n.d.). ScotClans. https://www.scotclans.com/pages/iron-age-celts-picts-and-romans

Israrkhan. (2021, June 16). *Scots trace their lineage to Egyptian Queen Scotia—yths and reality.* Medium. https://medium.com/lessons-from-history/scots-trace-their-lineage-to-egyptian-queen-scotia-myths-and-reality-5e8bbbd33310

James Stewart, 1st earl of Moray. (n.d.). Undiscovered Scotland. https://www.undiscoveredscotland.co.uk/usbiography/s/jamesst ewartmoray.html

James VI and I: Life story – Chapter 3: Regents. (n.d.). Tudor Times. https://www.tudortimes.co.uk/people/james-vi-i-life-story/regents

James VI and I: Life Story – Chapter 4: Coming of age. (n.d.). Tudor Times. https://www.tudortimes.co.uk/people/james-vi-i-life-story/coming-of-age

James VII (1633–1701). (n.d.). National Library of Scotland. https://www.nls.uk/exhibitions/jacobites/james-vii/

Jill, Duchess of Hamilton. (2010, August 13). *Benedict XVI should address the papacy's treatment of Robert the Bruce*. Catholic Herald. https://catholicherald.co.uk/benedict-xvi-should-address-the-papacys-treatment-of-robert-the-bruce/

Johnson, B. (n.d.-a). *Queen Anne*. Historic UK. https://www.historic-uk.com/HistoryUK/HistoryofBritain/Queen-Anne/

Johnson, B. (n.d.-b). *The Anglo-Scottish Wars (or Wars of Scottish Independence*. Historic UK. https://www.historic-uk.com/HistoryUK/HistoryofScotland/The-AngloScottish-Wars-or-Wars-of-Scottish-Independence/

Johnson, B. (n.d.-c). *The Darien scheme*. Historic UK. https://www.historic-uk.com/HistoryUK/HistoryofScotland/The-Darien-Scheme/

Johnson, B. (n.d.-d). *The Jacobite revolts: Chronology*. Historic UK. https://www.historic-uk.com/HistoryUK/HistoryofScotland/The-Jacobite-Revolts-Chronology/

Kennedy, L. (2019, October 21). *The prehistoric ages: How humans lived before written records*. History. https://www.history.com/news/prehistoric-ages-timeline#:~:text=In%20the%20Paleolithic%20period%20(roughl y

Kenneth II (971–995). (n.d.). ScotClans. https://www.scotclans.com/pages/kenneth-ii-971-995

Kessler, P. L. (n.d.). *Rheged (Recet)*. The History Files. https://www.historyfiles.co.uk/KingListsBritain/BritainRheged.htm

Kinclaven Castle, Perthshire. (n.d.). Castle Finders. https://castle-finders.co.uk/Scotland/kinclaven-castle.html

King Charles II | The public and personal life of a British monarch. (n.d.). Royal Museums Greenwich. https://www.rmg.co.uk/stories/topics/king-charles-ii-public-personal-life-british-monarch#:~:text=Venue%20hire-

King Culen. (n.d.). Undiscovered Scotland. https://www.undiscoveredscotland.co.uk/usbiography/monarchs/culen.html

King Eochaid and King Giric. (n.d.). Undiscovered Scotland. https://www.undiscoveredscotland.co.uk/usbiography/monarchs/eochaidgiric.html

King Indulf. (n.d.). Undiscovered Scotland. https://www.undiscoveredscotland.co.uk/usbiography/monarchs/indulf.html

Kinnatellus, king of Scotland (574–5). (n.d.). Royal Collection Trust. https://www.rct.uk/collection/403274/kinnatellus-king-of-scotland-574-5

Late Modern Period | History, timeline, and significant events. (2023, March 12). https://study.com/academy/lesson/late-modern-period-history-timeline-significant-events.html.

List of child brides. (2023). Wikipedia. https://en.wikipedia.org/wiki/List_of_child_brides

Local authority areas in Scotland. (n.d.). The Scottish Government. https://www.gov.scot/binaries/content/gallery/publications/statistics-publication/2015/02/scottish-local-government-financial-statistics-2013-14/00471983.gif

Lulach (The Fool) (1057–1058). (n.d.). ScotClans. https://www.scotclans.com/pages/lulach-the-fool-1057-1058

Mac, E. (2011, April 15). *Luguwalos: Carlisle's ancient roots.* Esmeralda's Cumbrian History & Folklore. https://esmeraldamac.wordpress.com/2011/04/15/carlisles-ancient-british-heritage-luguwalos/

MacInnes, A. (1990, May). *Covenanting Revolution and municipal enterprise.* History Today. https://www.historytoday.com/archive/covenanting-revolution-and-municipal-enterprise

MacInnes, I. A. (n.d.). *Scotland's second war of independence, 1332–1357.* Boydell and Brewer.

https://boydellandbrewer.com/9781783271443/scotlands-second-war-of-independence-1332-1357/#:~:text=The%20Second%20Scottish%20War%20of,Scottish%20crown%20recommenced%20once%20more

Maeatae. (2017, January 8). Eagles and Dragons Publishing. https://eaglesanddragonspublishing.com/tag/maeatae/

Maldonado, A. (2020, July 21). *Looting Scotland in the Viking age.* National Museums Scotland. https://blog.nms.ac.uk/2020/07/21/looting-scotland-in-the-viking-age/#:~:text=In%20795%20AD%20one%20of

Manning, R. B. (2006, May). *An Apprenticeship in Arms: The Origins of the British Army 1585–1702.* Oxford Academic

Manning, S. (2023). *Battle of Bannockburn.* Britannica. https://www.britannica.com/event/Battle-of-Bannockburn

McGraw, J. (n.d.). *The easiest guide to Scotland's archaeological time periods and ages.* Dig It! https://www.digitscotland.com/an-easy-guide-to-scotlands-archaeological-time-periods-and-ages/#:~:text=When%20was%20the%20Iron%20Age

McNeil, G. P. (2022, April 28). *Scota, queen of the Gadelians {fictitious}.* Geni. https://www.geni.com/people/Scota-Queen-of-the-Gadelians-fictitious/6000000000077265812

Morrill, J. S. (2023a). *Margaret Tudor.* Britannica. https://www.britannica.com/biography/Margaret-Tudor

Morrill, J. S. (2023b). *James V.* Britannica. https://www.britannica.com/biography/James-V

Neolithic farmers and monument builders. (n.d.). ScotClans. https://www.scotclans.com/pages/neolithic-farmers-and-monument-builders

Novantae Celtic tribe. (n.d.). Roman Britain. https://www.roman-britain.co.uk/tribes/novantae/

Ohlmeyer, J. H. (2023). *English civil wars.* Britannica. https://www.britannica.com/event/English-Civil-Wars

Parker, N. G. (2022). *Battle of Dunbar.* Britannica. https://www.britannica.com/event/Battle-of-Dunbar

Parrott-Sheffer, C. (2023). *James Stewart, 1st earl of Moray.* Britannica. https://www.britannica.com/biography/James-Stewart-1st-Earl-of-Moray

Parrott-Sheffer, C. (2023, February 21). *Pict.* Britannica. https://www.britannica.com/topic/Pict

Paxton, J. (2020, May 7). *Roman conquest of Britain: Caesar's expedition to Hadrian's Wall*. Wondrium Daily. https://www.wondriumdaily.com/roman-conquest-of-britain-caesars-expedition-to-hadrians-wall/#:~:text=So%2C%20Romans%20first%20encountered%20Britain

Pettit, H., Weston, P. (2018, June 4). *Exclusive: What Britain looked like during the last ice age: Interactive map reveals where ice corridors and glacial lakes formed 22,000 years ago*. MailOnline. https://www.dailymail.co.uk/sciencetech/article-5803855/Interactive-map-reveals-Britain-looked-like-ice-age.html

Prehistoric Scotland. (n.d.). ScotClans. https://www.scotclans.com/pages/prehistoric-scotland

Readman, K. (2021, April 25). *The first Scottish war of independence: Robert the Bruce vs Edward I*. The Collector. https://www.thecollector.com/the-first-scottish-war-of-independence-robert-the-bruce-vs-edward-i/

Reid, B. (n.d.). *The Siege of Stirling Castle*. Hidden Scotland. https://hiddenscotland.co/the-siege-of-stirling-castle/

Reid, B. (n.d.). *The Siege of Caerlaverock Castle*. Hidden Scotland. https://hiddenscotland.co/the-siege-of-caerlaverock-castle/

Renaissance and Reformation – Introduction. (n.d.). BBC. https://www.bbc.co.uk/history/scottishhistory/renaissance/intro_renaissance.shtml

Renaissance. (n.d.). National Galleries Scotland. https://www.nationalgalleries.org/art-and-artists/glossary-terms/renaissance

Restoration. (n.d.). UK Parliament. https://www.parliament.uk/about/living-heritage/evolutionofparliament/legislativescrutiny/act-of-union-1707/overview/restoration/

Revolution and civil war. (n.d.). UK Parliament. https://www.parliament.uk/about/living-heritage/evolutionofparliament/legislativescrutiny/act-of-union-1707/overview/revolution-and-civil-war/

Ring hill, fort. (n.d.). Ancient Monuments. https://ancientmonuments.uk/126000-ring-hill-fort-mid-galloway-and-wigtown-west-ward#.ZBhL5exBxQI

Roller, S. (2020, October 14). *6 key battles in the Wars of Scottish Independence*. History Hit. https://www.historyhit.com/key-battles-in-the-wars-of-scottish-independence/

Romans in Scotland. (n.d.). Travel Scotland. https://www.scotland.org.uk/history/romans-in-scotland

Roseveare, H. G. (2023). *Charles II*. Britannica. https://www.britannica.com/biography/Charles-II-king-of-Great-Britain-and-Ireland

Savage, L. R. (n.d.). *John Knox and the Scottish Reformation*. Historic UK. https://www.historic-uk.com/HistoryUK/HistoryofScotland/John-Knox-Scottish-Reformation/

Scottish battles and conflicts timeline. (n.d.). orgfree.com. http://skyelander.orgfree.com/sbattles.html

Scottish battles – the Second War of Scottish Independence. (n.d.). Scots Connection. https://www.scotsconnection.com/t-battles4.aspx

Selgovae Celtic tribe. (n.d.). Roman Britain. https://www.roman-britain.co.uk/tribes/selgovae/

Siege of Dundee (1651). (n.d.). Military Wiki. https://military-history.fandom.com/wiki/Siege_of_Dundee_(1651)

Siege of Haddington. (2021, April 26). Military Wiki. https://military-history.fandom.com/wiki/Siege_of_Haddington

Significant battles in Scottish history – Preston to Culloden. (n.d.). Scots Connection. https://www.scotsconnection.com/t-battles9.aspx

1603 – The Union Of The Crowns. (n.d.). ScotClans. https://www.scotclans.com/pages/1603-the-union-of-the-crowns

Snow, D. R. (2001). *Scotland's Irish origins*. Archeology Archive. https://archive.archaeology.org/0107/abstracts/scotland.html

Solly, M. (2020, January 30). *A not-so-brief history of Scottish independence*. Smithsonian Magazine. https://www.smithsonianmag.com/history/brief-history-scottish-independence-180973928/

Stirling Castle. (2023). Historic Environment Scotland. https://www.historicenvironment.scot/visit-a-place/places/stirling-castle/history/#:~:text=Stirling%20Castle%20has%20been%20likened

Succession problem: Edward I and the decision at Norham. (n.d.). BBC
Bitesize.
https://www.bbc.co.uk/bitesize/guides/zrxcwmn/revision/4#:
~:text=The%20Guardians%20invited%20Edward%20to

Succession problem: The Great Cause and Edward's choice. (n.d.). BBC
Bitesize.
https://www.bbc.co.uk/bitesize/guides/zrxcwmn/revision/6#:
~:text=Edward%20I%20chose%20John%20Balliol

Sundberg, A. (2022). Natural Disaster at the Closing of the Dutch
Golden Age . Cambridge University Press.

The Auld Alliance. (n.d.). Historic UK. https://www.historic-
uk.com/HistoryUK/HistoryofScotland/The-Auld-Alliance-
France-Scotland/

The Battle of Dunbar, 1296. (n.d.). BBC Bitesize.
https://www.bbc.co.uk/bitesize/topics/z8g86sg/articles/zh3fmf
r

The Battle of Inverlochy: February 2, 1645. (n.d.). Clan Cameron Online.
http://www.clan-cameron.org/battles/1645.html

The Britons of Strathclyde. (n.d.). English Monarchs.
https://www.englishmonarchs.co.uk/britons.html

The Bruces and the Balliols. (n.d.). Undiscovered Scotland.
https://www.undiscoveredscotland.co.uk/usbiography/monarch
s/balliolsbruces.html

The Caledonii tribe. (n.d.). The Romans in Britain.
https://www.romanobritain.org/4-celt/clb_tribe_caledonii.php

The Declaration of Arbroath. (n.d.). National Records of Scotland.
https://www.nrscotland.gov.uk/Declaration#:~:text=The%20D
eclaration%20is%20a%20letter

The Editors of Encyclopaedia Britannica. (n.d.). *Alba.* Britannica.
https://www.britannica.com/place/Alba-historical-kingdom-
Scotland

The Editors of Encyclopaedia Britannica. (n.d.). *Kenneth I.* Britannica.
https://www.britannica.com/biography/Kenneth-I

The Editors of Encyclopaedia Britannica. (2018). *Constantine I.*
Britannica. https://www.britannica.com/biography/Constantine-
I-king-of-Scotland

The Editors of Encyclopaedia Britannica. (2018). *Donald Bane.*
Britannica. https://www.britannica.com/place/Dalriada

The Editors of Encyclopaedia Britannica. (2018). *Dalriada*. Britannica. https://www.britannica.com/biography/Donald-Bane

The Editors of Encyclopaedia Britannica. (2018). *Kings and queens of Scotland*. Britannica. https://www.britannica.com/topic/Kings-and-Queens-of-Scotland-1856934

The Editors of Encyclopaedia Britannica. (2018). *Scot*. Britannica. https://www.britannica.com/topic/Scot

The Editors of Encyclopaedia Britannica. (2018, December 21). *Strathclyde*. Britannica. https://www.britannica.com/place/Strathclyde

The Editors of Encyclopaedia Britannica. (2019, July 15). *Lothian*. Britannica. https://www.britannica.com/place/Lothian

The Editors of Encyclopaedia Britannica. (2020). *Wessex*. Britannica. https://www.britannica.com/place/Wessex-historical-kingdom

The Editors of Encyclopaedia Britannica. (2022). *Alexander III*. Britannica. https://www.britannica.com/biography/Alexander-III-king-of-Scotland

The Editors of Encyclopaedia Britannica. (2022). *Balliol family*. Britannica. https://www.britannica.com/topic/Balliol-family

The Editors of Encyclopaedia Britannica. (2022). *David I*. Britannica. https://www.britannica.com/biography/David-I

The Editors of Encyclopaedia Britannica. (2022). *Duncan I*. Britannica. https://www.britannica.com/biography/Duncan-I

The Editors of Encyclopaedia Britannica. (2022). *George I*. Britannica. https://www.britannica.com/biography/George-I-king-of-Great-Britain

The Editors of Encyclopaedia Britannica. (2022). *Heptarchy*. Britannica. https://www.britannica.com/topic/Heptarchy

The Editors of Encyclopaedia Britannica. (2022). *James II*. Britannica. https://www.britannica.com/biography/James-II-king-of-Scotland

The Editors of Encyclopaedia Britannica. (2022). *James III*. Britannica. https://www.britannica.com/biography/James-III-king-of-Scotland

The Editors of Encyclopaedia Britannica. (2022). *John*. Britannica. https://www.britannica.com/biography/John-king-of-Scotland-1250-1313

The Editors of Encyclopaedia Britannica. (2022). *John Stewart, 2nd duke of Albany*. Britannica.

https://www.britannica.com/biography/John-Stewart-2nd-duke-of-Albany

The Editors of Encyclopaedia Britannica. (2022). *Malcolm II.* Britannica. https://www.britannica.com/biography/Malcolm-II

The Editors of Encyclopaedia Britannica. (2022). *Malcolm IV.* Britannica. https://www.britannica.com/biography/Malcolm-IV

The Editors of Encyclopaedia Britannica. (2022). *Mary of Lorraine.* Britannica. https://www.britannica.com/biography/Mary-of-Lorraine

The Editors of Encyclopaedia Britannica. (2022). *Michael III Canmore.* Britannica. https://www.britannica.com/biography/Malcolm-III-Canmore

The Editors of Encyclopaedia Britannica. (2022, August 28). *Margaret.* Britannica. https://www.britannica.com/biography/Margaret-queen-of-Scotland

The Editors of Encyclopaedia Britannica. (2023). *Archibald Douglas, 6th earl of Angus.* Britannica. https://www.britannica.com/biography/Alexander-I-king-of-Scotland

The Editors of Encyclopaedia Britannica. (2023). *Charles Edward, the young pretender.* Britannica. https://www.britannica.com/biography/Charles-Edward-the-Young-Pretender

The Editors of Encyclopaedia Britannica. (2023). *Constantine III.* Britannica. https://www.britannica.com/biography/Constantine-III-king-of-Scotland

The Editors of Encyclopaedia Britannica. (2023). *David II.* Britannica. https://www.britannica.com/biography/David-II

The Editors of Encyclopaedia Britannica. (2023). *Donald II.* Britannica. https://www.britannica.com/biography/Donald-II

The Editors of Encyclopaedia Britannica. (2023). *Edward: King of Scotland.* Britannica. https://www.britannica.com/biography/Edward-king-of-Scotland

The Editors of Encyclopaedia Britannica. (2023). *James I.* Britannica. https://www.britannica.com/biography/James-I-king-of-Scotland

The Editors of Encyclopaedia Britannica. (2023). *James IV*. Britannica. https://www.britannica.com/biography/James-IV-king-of-Scotland

The Editors of Encyclopaedia Britannica. (2023). *Kenneth III*. Britannica. https://www.britannica.com/biography/Kenneth-III

The Editors of Encyclopaedia Britannica. (2023). *Macbeth*. Britannica. https://www.britannica.com/biography/Macbeth-king-of-Scots

The Editors of Encyclopaedia Britannica. (2023). *Malcolm I*. Britannica. britannica.com/biography/Malcolm-I

The Editors of Encyclopaedia Britannica. (2023). *Robert II*. Britannica. https://www.britannica.com/biography/Robert-II-king-of-Scotland

The Editors of Encyclopaedia Britannica. (2023). *Robert III*. Britannica. https://www.britannica.com/biography/Robert-III

The Editors of Encyclopaedia Britannica. (2023). *William I*. Britannica. https://www.britannica.com/biography/William-I-king-of-Scotland

The Editors of Encyclopaedia Britannica. (2023, January 1). *Constantine II*. Britannica. https://www.britannica.com/biography/Constantine-II-king-of-Scotland

The Editors of Encyclopaedia Britannica. (2023, February 27). *Caledonia*. Britannica. https://www.britannica.com/place/Caledonia-ancient-region-Britain

The Editors of Encyclopaedia Britannica. (2023, March 28). *Alexander I*. Britannica. https://www.britannica.com/biography/Alexander-I-king-of-Scotland

The Enlightenment and Industrial Revolution – the Industrial Revolution. (n.d.). BBC. https://www.bbc.co.uk/history/scottishhistory/enlightenment/features_enlightenment_industry.shtml

The first hunter gatherers. (n.d.). ScotClans. https://www.scotclans.com/pages/the-first-hunter-gatherers

The Highland Clearances. (n.d.). Scottish History Society. https://scottishhistorysociety.com/the-highland-clearances/

The kingdom of the Angles. (n.d.). BBC. https://www.bbc.co.uk/scotland/history/articles/kingdom_of_t

he_angles/#:~:text=The%20Angles%20were%20Germanic%20i
nvaders

The kingdom of the Britons. (n.d.). BBC.
https://www.bbc.co.uk/scotland/history/articles/kingdom_of_t
he_britons/

The Newsroom. (2017, March 1). *Roslin 1303: Scotland's forgotten battle.*
The Scotsman. https://www.scotsman.com/whats-on/arts-and-
entertainment/roslin-1303-scotlands-forgotten-battle-604343

The Romans in Scotland. (n.d.). National Museums Scotland.
https://www.nms.ac.uk/explore-our-collections/stories/scottish-
history-and-archaeology/the-romans-in-scotland/

The Scotti. (n.d.). British Isles: Past and Present.
https://www.islandguide.co.uk/history/scotti.htm

The Scottish diaspora: How Scots spread across the globe. (2016, January 25).
The Scotsman. https://www.scotsman.com/whats-on/arts-and-
entertainment/scottish-diaspora-how-scots-spread-across-globe-
1484633

The Scottish Reformation. (n.d.). BBC.
https://www.bbc.co.uk/scotland/history/articles/scottish_refor
mation/#:~:text=The%20Reformation%20split%20the%20Chur
ch

The Scottish Reformation, c.1525–1560. (n.d.). The Scottish History
Society. https://scottishhistorysociety.com/the-scottish-
reformation-c-1525-1560/

The Selgovae tribe. (n.d.). The Romans in Britain.
https://www.romanobritain.org/4-celt/clb_tribe_selgovae.php

The Stewarts. (n.d.). The Royal Family. https://www.royal.uk/stewarts-
0#:~:text=The%20Stewart%20dynasty%20descended%20from,fl
ourished%20for%20over%20three%20centuries

The Taexali tribe. (n.d.). The Romans in Britain.
https://www.romanobritain.org/4-celt/clb_tribe_taexali.php

The Treaty of Edinburgh-Northampton, 1328. (n.d.). Scottish Archives for
Schools.
https://www.scottisharchivesforschools.org/WarsOfIndependen
ce/Edinburgh-Northampton.asp

The Union of 1603. (n.d.). The Scottish History Society.
https://scottishhistorysociety.com/the-union-of-1603/

The Vacomagi tribe. (n.d.). The Romans in Britain.
https://www.romanobritain.org/4-celt/clb_tribe_vacomagi.php

The Venicones tribe. (n.d.). The Romans in Britain.
    https://www.romanobritain.org/4-celt/clb_tribe_venicones.php
The Wars of Independence. (n.d.). The Scottish History Society.
    https://scottishhistorysociety.com/the-wars-of-independence/
Tikkanen, A. (2022). *Robert Stewart, 1st duke of Albany.* Britannica.
    https://www.britannica.com/biography/Robert-Stewart-1st-
    duke-of-Albany
Toolis, R. (2022, February 27). *Beyond the wall: exploring the prehistoric
    origins of Scotland.* The Past. https://the-past.com/feature/beyond-
    the-wall-exploring-the-prehistoric-origins-of-scotland/
Union between Scotland and England? (n.d.). UK Parliament.
    https://www.parliament.uk/about/living-
    heritage/evolutionofparliament/legislativescrutiny/act-of-union-
    1707/overview/union-between-scotland-and-england/
Union of the crowns. (n.d.). UK Parliament.
    https://www.parliament.uk/about/living-
    heritage/evolutionofparliament/legislativescrutiny/act-of-union-
    1707/overview/union-of-the-
    crowns/#:~:text=Because%20the%20Queen%20had%20died,a
    %20union%20of%20the%20crowns.
Votadini Celtic tribe. (n.d.). Roman Britain. https://www.roman-
    britain.co.uk/tribes/votadini/
Webster, B. (2022). *Robert the Bruce.* Britannica.
    https://www.britannica.com/biography/Robert-the-Bruce
What is a crannog? (n.d.). The Scottish Crannog Centre.
    https://crannog.co.uk/what-is-a-
    crannog/#:~:text=Crannogs%20are%20found%20across%20Sc
    otland
Who were the nine tribes of ancient Scotland? (2016, October 25). The
    Scotsman. https://www.scotsman.com/whats-on/arts-and-
    entertainment/who-were-nine-tribes-ancient-scotland-865992
Wiener, J. (2018). *Scota: Mother of the Scottish people.* World History Et
    Cetera. https://etc.worldhistory.org/uncategorized/scota-
    mother-of-the-scottish-people/
Wolff, A. (2023). *Edgar.* Britannica.
    https://www.britannica.com/biography/Edgar-king-of-Scotland
Yodamo. (2021, February 13). *B.C. 1526–1513: Thutmose, Gaythelos and
    Scota.* The Chisper Effect.

https://chisper256891285.wordpress.com/2021/02/13/b-c-1526-1513-thutmose-gaythelos-scota/

FREE BONUS FROM HBA: EBOOK BUNDLE

Greetings!

First of all, thank you for reading our books. As fellow passionate readers of History and Mythology, we aim to create the very best books for our readers.

Now, we invite you to join our VIP list. As a welcome gift, we offer the History & Mythology Ebook Bundle below for free. Plus you can be the first to receive new books and exclusives! Remember it's 100% free to join.

Simply scan the QR code to join.

For Kids:

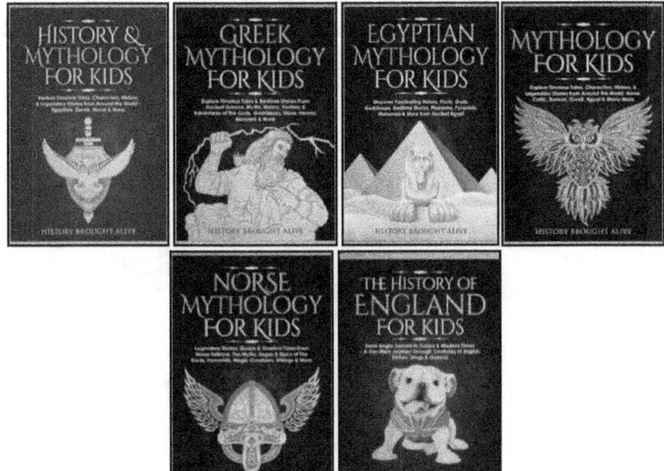

HISTORY OF SCOTLAND

We sincerely hope you enjoyed our new book *"History of Scotland"*. We would greatly appreciate your feedback with an honest review at the place of purchase.

First and foremost, we are always looking to grow and improve as a team. It is reassuring to hear what works, as well as receive constructive feedback on what should improve. Second, starting out as an unknown author is exceedingly difficult, and Amazon reviews go a long way toward making the journey out of anonymity possible. Please take a few minutes to write an honest review.

Best regards,

History Brought Alive

http://historybroughtalive.com/